THE
STREET
ADDICT
ROLE

SUNY Series, The New Inequalities

Anthony Gary Dworkin, Editor

THE
STREET
ADDICT
ROLE

A THEORY OF HEROIN ADDICTION

Richard C. Stephens

State University of New York Press

Published by
State University of New York Press, Albany

© 1991   State University of New York

All rights reserved

Printed in the United States of America

For information, address the State University of New York Press,
State University Plaza, Albany, NY 12246

Production by Christine M. Lynch
Marketing by Theresa A. Swierzowski

Library of Congress Cataloging-in-Publication Data

Stephens, Richard C.
    The street addict role :   a theory of heroin addiction /   Richard C.
Stephens.
        p.   cm. — (SUNY series, The new inequalities)
    Includes bibliographical references and index.
    ISBN 0-7914-0619-9
    ISBN 0-7914-0620-2 (pbk)
    1. Heroin habit—United States.   2. Narcotic addicts—United
States—Psychology.   3. Drug abuse—United States.   4. Social role—
United States.   5. Symbolic interactionism.   I. Title.
II. Series: SUNY series in the new inequalities.
HV5825.S743   1991
362.29'3'0973—dc20   90–39205
                                                                   CIP

10   9   8   7   6   5   4   3   2

To

John A. O'Donnell, Ph.D.

1916–1979

Contents

Foreword

No terms are more confusing, or misleading, than "drugs," "drug users," or "under the influence of drugs." Although widely used in the media and in discussion, these terms actually refer to a tremendous variety of often disparate drugs. As Stephens points out, they differ in the substance used, the expectations of what effect they will produce, and the immediate environment in which they are taken. The range of substances used is wide: alcohol, nicotine, hallucinogenic drugs like marijuana, stimulants like cocaine, mind-altering drugs, mood modifiers, and psychoactive narcotics such as heroin that affect the central nervous system and influence mood behavior and perception through action on the brain. Narcotics include opium, morphine, codeine, and, primarily, heroin, a semi-synthetic opiate chemically processed from opium. People have used opium for thousands of years; in fact, opium was legal in the United States until early in the twentieth century whether it was smoked, taken as morphine or heroin.

Shephens' study focuses on contemporary American heroin use: He develops a theory of heroin addiction built around the ghetto street addict who constitutes nearly all present-day American users. Heroin is generally considered the hardest of the "hard drugs:" It is far more dangerous than cocaine. One can experience the "highs" of heroin by inhaling, smoking or, more commonly, by injecting it into the veins, the method closely identified with the street addict's way of life. Repeated heroin use increases tolerance, and the addict craves ever greater amounts to achieve the same effects. Withdrawal symptoms occur after some eight hours of abstinence—the eyes and nose water, perspiration becomes profuse, the body aches, and nausea and diarrhea occur.

Addiction to heroin, as exemplified by the street addict, is serious business. Life becomes an all encompassing rat race of copping and the constant daily hassle to support the habit. Stephens has well summed up this life style: "In a typical career, the addict

ix

often climbs to the heights of ecstasy and self-satisfaction only to plummet to great despair. At one moment the junkie is 'taking care of business'—leading an exciting eventful life filled with rewards of drugs, material goods and status among peers. In the next instance, however, the habit becomes unmanageably large, expensive, and the descent to the level of the 'greasy dope fiend' begins."

The addict commits an enormous amount of crime, sometimes in the daily search for funds to support the habit and to survive. Primarily, addicts engage in drug dealing and theft, but they also engage in illegal gambling, forgery, and various con games. Arrest is always a possibility for them, and physically they become more and more debilitated and more susceptible to disease due to poor eating and living style habits. The greatest problem facing the addict is the possibility of acquiring the AIDS virus through the joint sharing of needles. In fact, heroin use has become one of the chief ways in which AIDS is spread heterosexually. Even prior to the AIDS epidemic the age-adjusted death rates for heroin addicts were estimated to be two to four times greater than expected.

Many years ago Ernest W. Burgess, the distinguished University of Chicago sociologist, was asked what advice he would give to a young sociologist. He replied that one should select a limited sociological problem and devote one's life to it. This is precisely what Richard Stephens has done. Beginning in 1971 with his Wisconsin doctoral dissertation, "Relapse among Narcotic Addicts: An Empirical Test of Labeling Theory," Stephens has devoted nearly twenty years to the research of various sociological aspects of heroin addiction. In all he has published a book on mind-altering drugs, numerous chapters in books related to drug use, over 35 articles, and he has received six large research grants, the most recent one $2.6 million for a study of AIDS education for IV heroin users and their sexual partners. He has served on numerous national committees dealing with drug use.

To this book Stephens brings extensive research, as well as knowledge and insights acquired over many years. The book reveals an intellectual depth and sociological imagination not often encountered in contemporary sociological research. Moreover, he is an applied sociologist in a discipline that, unfortunately, largely avoids dealing with the issues of the "real world." His work, as well as his conclusions, differ markedly from those of Alfred Lindesmith, whose sociological theory of opiate addiction became a classic. Lindesmith focused on the individual addict, using a combination of symbolic interactionism and learning theory. He concluded that the addict takes on the self-concept of his being a heroin addict when he recognizes the withdrawal symptoms that follow abstinence from heroin use. The drug becomes necessary to relieve his craving for it. In contrast, Stephens' primary concern has not been with individuals but with the group or the subcultural aspects of addiction. Persons in subcultures share a set of norms, values, and beliefs distinguishable from the society of which they are a part. Stephens finds this reflected in the "street addict" of our inner city areas. As he points out, the addicts' "self concept, their sense of personal worth and their status in the addict sub-culture all revolve around this role" of being a street addict. They interact with one another. Due to these subcultural influences, he finds that the addicts use heroin not necessarily to counter the pain suffered by withdrawal, as Lindesmith maintained, but in order to experience the euphoria of drug use "highs" in themselves.

For some time sociological research has shown that heroin addiction involves a process of learning in association with others, including learning how to administer the drug and how to appreciate its effects. Building on these findings, Stephens has sought to explain two sets of facts. First nearly all of today's regular heroin users come from the inner cities of our large urban areas. They are generally young, male, members of minority groups, under-employed, and educationally disadvantaged. The second set of facts is that even though about 500,00 persons are addicted to heroin and are regular users, there is also a much larger group of occasional users or "chippers" whom Trebach has estimated to be as high as 3.5 million. This large number suggests that the addiction process may not result simply in taking the drug but may involve other factors of a group nature.

In his research, Stephens not only has made use of sophisticated quantitative research techniques but, unlike many of his sociological contemporaries, he has relied on strong theoretical and qualitative methods of research. At the outset he fully explains his analytical framework and the premises. He views street heroin use as being woven into the social or sociocultural context of the inner city life and an addict subculture. The processes that produce the deviant behavior of heroin users do not differ inherently from those that produce non-deviants. In other words, the subprocess affecting deviants operates within the same general framework of human behavior.

The theoretical perspective of his research is heavily grounded in symbolic interaction and role theory, concepts basically developed by George Herbert Mead and Herbert Blumer. These concepts encompass all human behavior, both deviant and non-deviant alike. Social behavior develops not only as we respond to the expectations of others and as we experience their norms, but also through processes of social interaction as we anticipate the responses of other people to us and then incorporate them into our conduct patterns. In applying this theory to deviant behavior, one must consider the self-identity of deviants and the processes of socialization into a deviant role. The use of heroin does not necessarily make one actually a deviant; a person becomes a deviant by playing a social role that exhibits distinctive normative behavior in a disapproved direction.

A deviant identity is derived from interacting with others and, in turn, with others' reaction to him. Such social roles represent structured behavioral expectations so that the goal is not to understand role interaction processes in individual heroin addicts but to "understand the general and regularly predictable behavior of a group of individuals defined by their roles." Involved in this behavior development are the processes by which persons acquire the skills, knowledge, attitudes, values, and motives needed for the performance of a street addict role. Their addiction is basically role-playing and it is as much a commitment to a life style as it is dependency on a drug—to a life style as much as to a substance. Occasional users, the "chippers," can be explained as persons who have not yet committed themselves to the addict life style.

Examining the sociological literature on heroin use, including his own research in the field, Stephens found support for his own views on the importance and nature of the street addict role. He concluded that a correlation exists between the values of the subculture of the street society and addict role requirements and that persons committed to a street addict role are more likely to be regular users of heroin. Evidence also exists of a close correlation between pre-existing roles and the street addict role, thus facilitating the socialization into the street addict role. He found that relapses into drug use are definitely related to the degree of commitment to a street addict role and that role strain and role conflict are significantly related to a person's desire to become abstinent.

Stephens claims that street addicts are "rational actors" to the extent that most of them choose to become street addicts and to adopt the role appropriate to the addict's way of life. Street addicts are products of areas where there are limited opportunities for success in the outside world. Persons who live in these areas regard heroin use as an "expressiveness lifestyle which gives dignity and a sense of belonging and success to many alienated and disfranchised individuals." He terms such a role as a "cool cat syndrome," a favorable attitude toward conning or tricking others and an antisocial attitude toward the world outside their own group. The "cool cat" displays little concern or guilt for his actions. Rather, he values signs of material success, such as possession of heroin and other drugs. He admires and practices an ability to communicate readily in street language and to experience its excitement. His role consists of not believing in long-range planning, in condemning snitching, and in minimizing the employment of violence. Deriving his role from the street addict culture, the addict puts a high premium on the ability to con, tricking others to provide drugs, money, food, or lodging. Finally, the street addict role involves feelings of persecution in a world largely peopled by those he cannot trust.

Such a view of heroin addiction is consistently in contradiction to the widely held position that heroin addiction arises from individualistic physiological or genetic factors or personality adjustment difficulties. Practitioners in fields of medicine, psychiatry, or clinical psychology largely believe that addicts suffer from some type of "mental illness" or personality disorder and are "sick." Being "emotionally ill," such persons should receive professional individualized treatment. This reasoning often is circular in the sense that a person is supposed originally to take heroin because he is emotionally disturbed, which is proved because he continued

continued to use it. Stephens' approach is that heroin use is not an "escape" in psychological terms, nor is it "retreatist" in terms of Robert Merton's anomie theory. Rather, socioculturally heroin use is a measure of involvement. "A badge of membership in a close-knit society." Moreover, it is illogical to believe that a heroin "high," powerfully rewarding in itself, and so brief, could be the reason "sick" persons seek the drug.

In discussing users and non-users, Stephens points out that those who choose to use heroin already possess prior roles and a self-concept that are congruent with the street addict role. The first use situation is theoretically significant as it involves opportunity, availability of the drug, and social support. In fact, first use is, most likely, the result of peer pressure or curiosity, although it also can be a "rational" active pursuit of street addict life. After a "honeymoon phase" of euphoria, the addict becomes "hooked." The street addict identity and role are then achieved, which is followed by isolation and closure, an increasing involvement in a deviant life style in which the junkie self-identity becomes more conferred, helped in part by the labeling of others. "The world of the street addict is a catch-as-catch-can melange of activities designed to assure an adequate supply of money for drugs and secondly to provide for all other living expenses." The addict is likely to continue this role playing, although a conflict of roles may arise if the role demand of copping or hustling become either too difficult or are in major conflict with previous or emerging roles. All this may lead the addict to abandon the street addict role and seek abstinence through treatment or through other means.

Sociologists have become notorious for conducting social research that, in the final analysis offers few or no suggestions as to the studies' practical implications. It is largely for this reason that sociology often does not command the same degree of respect that do those in the fields of economics, psychology, and political science where frequently suggestions derived from their studies are incorporated into planning programs. Stephens is an exception: he is willing to state his opinions about what can be done in dealing with the street addict and the drug problem in general. He believes that any form of "treatment" offers a respite—a time to think about the addictive street life style. It also exposes the addict to others who are not dependent on drugs and that offers him the opportunity to explore alternative non-addict roles. At the same time, he is highly skeptical of programs that categorize heroin addicts as essentially "sick persons." Methadone maintenance as a substitute for heroin use has some merits, but it can lead to a substitution of one addictive drug for another. Therapeutic communities that stress self-help adult resocialization are most successful for those most committed to giving up the street addict life; because it is a demanding program, it would not work well for the average street addict. Stephens feels that to be effective, treatment programs must consider the larger social and cultural context in which the addict has operated. Resocialization and the adoption of new roles is a slow and arduous process, this treatment will work only with committed addicts.

As for the larger issues of controlling illegal drug use and users, Stephens believes that harsher penalties and strict enforcement will not work. The cost is prohibitive and the wide use of urine testing and seizure of private property are violations of the Bill of Rights. The coerced treatment of addicts is no more effective than are other approaches. Heroin maintenance programs, such as those carried out by medical clinics in Great Britain, have considerable merit, yet they do not deal with the underlying reasons for heroin use. Still, he advocates an experimental trial in the United States. Programs of drug interdiction at our borders are impractical. On the important and increasing question of legalization, Stephens advocates decriminalization as a program halfway between criminalization and legalization. Complete legalization would add to substance abuse and would signify that the government condones drug usage. Based on his theories and empirical research, Stephens advocates that, instead, the United States face up more fully to the problems presented by lower class inner city neighborhoods where heroin use is concentrated.

Because addicts are "rational actors" in their choice of the street life, they "need to learn in treatment, in interaction with others, and with societal agents that true and lasting change can only occur if they take responsibility for their own behavior." The higher incidence of seropositivity rates for AIDS in inner city areas has been an incentive to heroin addicts to come to grips with their addiction. It is "likely that most persons faced with a genuine chance of dying because of their behavior will attempt to change their behavior." At the same time, however, the street addict subculture has isolated the addict from conventional society. The only persons whom he is likely to know well are other addicts, and they tend to reinforce the addiction process rather than to provide positive social support for him to stay off drugs. Like other deviant subcultures, the street addict subculture does not prepare it members to reenter the conventional world; rather, it inhibits re-entry.

Marshall B. Clinard
Professor Emeritus of Sociology
University of Wisconsin—Madison

Preface

This book has long been in the making. In fact, in many ways it has taken me more than two decades to write it. The first kernels of the ideas expressed herein were developed when I started my career in drug abuse research as a Commissioned Officer in the United States Public Health Service at Lexington, Ky. in 1968. I was fortunate to be able to interact with some very good researchers there including John A. O'Donnell, Mike Agar, Carl Chambers and Bob Weppner. I began to believe that both the sociological and anthropological enterprises had many insights to contribute to understanding drug use in America. Further, in many spirited luncheon conversations and good natured debates with my psychiatric, social worker and clinical psychologist colleagues, I began more and more to doubt much of their explanation for this form of deviant behavior. Indeed, with a variety of colleagues, I began to write articles on the street addict role based on what I believe was a more sociologically and ethnographically informed perspective on this phenomenon. This belief was strengthened when I went to New York City as Deputy Director of Research for the New York Narcotics Addiction Control Commission. There working with Mike Agar, Doug Lipton, Ed Preble and others, I began even more to believe in the concept of the street addict role. And I began to write more and more about this belief.

At the same time a number of good ethnographic studies, all cited herein, continued to be produced. Increasingly, I felt the need to "tie" all of this work together, and, with the constant urging of Marshall B. Clinard and others, I began to write this book. The book has benefited from the advice and work of many. Marshall B. Clinard, Mike Agar, Sam Marullo, Thomas Feucht, Bill Morgan, Phil Manning, Christine Nocjar, Brian Gibbs, Barbara Stephens and others read portions of the book and suggested changes, many of which were incorporated. As always, however, I accept responsibility for any errors committed.

I have a great team of undergraduate research assistants who helped in the clerical tasks in writing this book including typing, bibliography searching, duplicating and all of the other myriad tasks. Special thanks go to the two Roebuck sisters, Theresa and Jennifer, to Amy Rice, Anthony Guido, and to Carmen Munoz. I would also like to thank my graduate assistants, T. Shawn Sullivan and Loretta Constantino-Crozier. They put up with my short deadlines and hyperkenetic personality. Thanks also go to Sheree Thomas and Charmaine Veselsky for their assistance early on in preparation of the book.

Very special thanks also go to Marshall B. Clinard, my former doctoral major professor and colleague for a quarter of a century. Marshall is that rare individual who continues to show interest in his students long after they have left the "nest." Since I left the University of Wisconsin in 1968 he directed my dissertation and then encouraged me in my endeavors throughout all of my career. I believe he is the only individual on earth to have suffered through reading all of my work. I shall be eternally grateful to him for his advice and friendship through all these years. In the spirit of the analytical framework of this book, he truly is for me a professional and personal role model.

This book is dedicated to another role model and a man about whom I think often. Dr. John A. O'Donnell was one of the most remarkable human beings I have ever met. He was my boss on my first professional job at Lexington, Ky. He took me, a fledgling social scientist, under his wing and showed me how to be a social researcher. His commitment to integrity and quality was undying. His analytical abilities were a joy to observe. Indeed, I always felt in awe of the incredible instrument that his mind was. He has enormous standing among the professionals in our field. But in addition he was a kind, considerate and enormously witty individual. His premature death was a personal blow to me and an immense loss to the drug abuse research field. I continue to miss him.

Finally, I want to thank my family: Barbara, my wife, Keturah, my daughter and Benjamin, my son. Their energies, humor, joie de vivre, accomplishments, understanding, and, most of all, love have made life worth living.

This book was written while I was supported, in part, by National Institute on Drug Abuse grants (R01DA05151 and R18DA05754).

Chapter One

Introduction

In the United States today, many citizens are concerned about what they perceive as the menace of a massive drug epidemic. In response, government at all levels has declared a "war on drugs." The President of the United States plans to spend billions of dollars on this offensive.

A new ominous phenomenon has arrived on the drug scene in America. This is the threat of AIDS. Intravenous drug users now constitute the second largest "at risk" group for contracting this always fatal disease. AIDS is easily acquired by sharing contaminated needles used for intravenous drug injections, a practice common among the addict population. Indeed, intravenous drug users are probably primarily responsible for spreading the disease to the heterosexual population through sexual contact with non-intravenous users. Many addicts engage in sexual intercourse with significant others who themselves do not use drugs. (Feucht, Stephens, and Roman, 1990). Many female addicts (and women, known as "strawberries," who trade sex for crack) engage in prostitution and thus can pass the virus on to their unsuspecting partners. Finally, women can transmit the disease to their unborn children; a majority of pediatric AIDS cases in the U.S. are accounted for by mothers who either themselves are intravenous users or are the sexual partners of users.

Given this great concern about AIDS and drug abuse, drug abuse researchers, practitioners, and lay persons ask the questions: "Why do people use heroin and other drugs? And why do they use them intravenously?" This book is an attempt to develop integrated and data-based answers to these questions. While the book addresses heroin use, I could just as easily focus on the use of many street

1

drugs (like "crack" and cocaine) and the intravenous route of administration as the chief phenomena to be explained. The emphasis on heroin use emerges partly from the autobiographical fact that I have devoted nearly two decades of my life to the study of its use. Also, many of the studies cited herein use narcotics addicts as their research subjects so that the knowledge base is better established for narcotic addiction than it is for some newer abuse patterns such as crack use.

As I will discuss in detail later in this book, most researchers and practitioners in the field favor explanations for heroin use which are based in the intrapsychic and interpersonal problems of the individual. This particular individualistic emphasis is due to the fact that for decades the field has been dominated by those trained in medicine, psychiatry and clinical psychology. Their explanations derive from the so-called disease models. Most typically, addicts are diagnosed as suffering from some form of "mental illness" or personality disorder. They often are labelled "character disorders" or "sociopaths." Certainly, their behavior is considered irrational and dangerous, both to themselves and others. Drug use is considered a symptom of some more fundamental underlying disorder. Persons use drugs to escape the problems they encounter in living. Some form of "individually tailored treatment" aimed at solving these problems is indicated.

Some sociologists and anthropologists, however, bring a different perspective to bear on narcotic addiction. Two of the most influential of these were Alfred Lindesmith and Ed Preble. Lindesmith (1968) viewed addiction as an extension of normal learning processes. Using a combination of symbolic interactionist and learning theory, Lindesmith described how persons come to look upon themselves as addicts. Ed Preble, (see for example, Preble and Casey [1969]; Preble and Miller [1977]) in both a series of articles and through his direct influence on a number of young ethnographers, came to view heroin addiction as a deviant lifestyle. He and a number of other ethnographically trained researchers study addicts in much the same way that anthropologists and participant observers studied primitive cultures and deviant subcultures in urban America. A crucial element in these studies was the abandonment of the concept of psychopathy.

Addicts were viewed as rather "normal" participants in a lifestyle, albeit a deviant one.

While a number of these studies have been conducted, they do not seem to have been guided by any one theoretical perspective. The main purpose of this book is to integrate these studies into just such a theoretically meaningful explanation. To accomplish this task, I shall draw heavily upon the symbolic interactionist and role theory perspectives. By combining the ethnographic insights with role theory/symbolic interactionism, I will develop what I call a "sociocultural explanation" of heroin addiction. The primary thesis of this book is that persons become socialized into the role of a street addict. They come to see themselves as street addicts and are viewed by others as street addicts. Their self concept, their sense of personal worth and their status in the addict subculture all revolve around this role. In short they become committed to a deviant existential identity.

A Heroin Primer

Before I take the reader on this theoretical journey, however, a small amount of fundamental knowledge about narcotics and related drugs needs to be understood. I shall briefly review the physiological, pharmacological, and other fundamentals of drug use. A number of texts (including Hofmann [1975], Leavitt [1982], Cox, et al. [1983] and Liska [1986]) discuss these issues in much more detail and the reader is referred to them.

Types of Psychoactive Drugs

Heroin and other narcotics belong to a class of chemicals known as psychoactive drugs. While these drugs have an impact on many different body systems, they primarily affect the central nervous system. That is, they influence mood, perception, and behavior through their actions on the brain. The psychoactive drugs in turn can be classified into a number of different categories. There are several different classificatory schema in use. One of the more popular is based on both pharmacological structures of the chemicals and their effects on the central nervous system. Using this scheme, the psychoactive substances are divided into the narcotics, the generalized depressants, the mood modifiers, the hallucinogens, and the stimulants.

The narcotics, the main focus of this book, in turn can be divided into three categories (1) naturally occurring opiates, which are directly derived from the opium poppy include opium, morphine and codeine; (2) semisynthetic opiates are drugs which are chemically processed from the opium plant; heroin is the most notable example of these; and (3) synthetic narcotics which are man-made and have chemical structures and physiological effects similar to the opiates. These include methadone and meperidine (Demerol). Narcotics are chiefly used legally in the treatment of pain. In fact, they remain the most effective pain control medications known to humankind. Heroin is highly euphoric, and it is this property which has led to its popularity on the street as an illegal drug.

The second major category of mind-altering drugs is the generalized depressants. Among these are the sedative and hypnotic drugs including secobarbital (Seconal), pentobarbital (Nembutal) and methaqualone (Quaalude); ethanol, or beverage alcohol; "minor" tranquilizers such as diazepoxide (Librium) and diazepam (Valium); and general anesthetic agents such as solvents, glue, gasoline, and amyl nitrite. In medical practice, many of the generalized depressants are used primarily to reduce anxiety and to induce sleep, although they may have other uses such as muscle relaxants. Outside of medical practice, these drugs are used by a large number of persons to get "high." The high is most often likened to the type of euphoria experienced with alcohol.

The third major category of drugs is the mood modifiers. They include the "major tranquilizers" such as Thorazine, the antidepressants such as Elavil, and the MAO inhibitors such as Nardil or Parnate. These drugs are not commonly abused on the streets.

The fourth category is the hallucinogens. These drugs include the psychedelics such as LSD, DMT, peyote, and mescaline. PCP, a sometimes popular animal tranquilizer called "angel dust," is also a hallucinogen. Probably the most widely used drug in this category is marihuana. These substances, as appropriately named, produce hallucinations, mood changes, and perceptual changes ranging from fairly dramatic (with LSD or PCP) to relatively mild (marihuana). With a few minor exceptions these drugs are not used in medicine. They are widely abused on the streets.

The fifth, and final, category is the stimulants. The stimulants include the true amphetamines such as methamphetamine (speed) and chemical analogs such as Preludin. Also included is the increasingly popular cocaine (and its freebased derivative crack). While in decades past amphetamines were widely prescribed by doctors as part of weight loss programs, few respected physicians do so today. With a few minor exceptions, the amphetamines are not utilized in medical practice today. However, they are widely used on the streets with cocaine in its several different forms being one of the current favorites. Very recent information indicates that methamphetamine, in the form of "crank" or "ice", is reemerging as an increasingly popular drug, as well.

Almost all of the psychoactive drugs, with the exception of the mood modifiers, are used on the streets today. Indeed street addicts, although primarily committed to heroin, will use a number of other substances; these users are often referred to as "poly-drug abusers." Almost all street addicts are regular users of cocaine (often combined with heroin in a concoction known as a "speedball"), marihuana, and alcohol.

Routes of Administration

The psychoactive substances can be brought into the body in a number of different ways. Heroin, in particular, can be used by virtually any route of administration. First, it can be "snorted," or inhaled through the nose. The heroin passes through the membranes of the nose into the nearby blood vessels and thence to the brain. Novice heroin users will often snort heroin before they move on to injecting the drug. Heroin can also be ingested through the mouth although this route is rarely, if ever, used. Heroin can be smoked, either by itself or sprinkled on a tobacco or marihuana cigarette. Smoking heroin was a common route of administration among American soldiers in Vietnam (Robins, 1973).

By far, the most common route of administration is injection. There are three techniques by which one can inject drugs. The first, and the one most often used medically (and coincidentally by physician and nurse addicts), is intramuscular injection. The drug is injected directly into the muscle. Street addicts rarely use this route. The second route is subcutaneous injection, where the needle is placed in tissue under the skin. This procedure is known on the streets as "skinpopping." Finally, there is intravenous injection, which is the route favored by most street addicts. Here the drug is injected directly into a vein thereby allowing the quickest and most direct route to the brain. This is the most efficient route, as well; one can get the most immediate and best "high" with the smallest amount of drug.

The Physiological Components of Heroin Use

There are several physiological aspects of heroin use which are essential to understanding this phenomenon. These are tolerance, withdrawal, and physical addiction. Tolerance is a process which applies to all narcotics. Basically, tolerance describes an adjustment process whereby the body requires increasingly larger amounts of drug to achieve the same effects. An example will make this clearer. A person may start out using one bag of heroin a day. The person gets "high" on this amount. After regular use (perhaps on a daily basis for a couple of weeks), the same high can no longer be achieved on this amount of drug; a larger quantity is needed. The process repeats itself with almost no upper limit on the amount of drug needed to get high. One part of the motivation in using increasing amounts of heroin is to continue to get that same desirable "high."

Related to tolerance is cross-tolerance. Cross-tolerance simply means that a person who is tolerant to a drug is also tolerant to an equivalent quantity of any other drug within that same pharmacological category. For instance, a person who is tolerant at a certain level to heroin would be tolerant to Dilaudid at an equivalent pharmacological level. This is the basis for methadone maintenance (about which I will have more to say later in this book.) Fundamentally, a person who is addicted to heroin can have that addiction "transferred" to methadone at a pharmacologically equivalent level.

The concepts of withdrawal and physical addiction are intimately interrelated. Basically, withdrawal is an indicator of physical addiction.[1] If a individual has used heroin several times a day for a period of two or three weeks, he or she in all likelihood has become physically addicted. That is the body has adjusted in such a fashion that the person "needs" the drug. The way in which the individual realizes this dependency is when he or she experiences the withdrawal syndrome. The heroin withdrawal or abstinence syndrome commences about eight hours after the last "fix" with watering of the eyes and nose, aches and pains escalating to the point of profuse sweating, severe nausea, vomiting, and diarrhea. In the later stage, the arms and legs may involuntarily twitch (thus giving rise to the expression "kicking the habit"), and the person is in a pretty sad state of affairs for a few days. The dramatic aspect of withdrawal is that these symptoms quickly disappear if narcotics are administered. Thus, withdrawal provides the "hook" in addiction, in that the addict knows that it will occur within eight hours following the last administration of the drug. The addict also knows that symptoms will disappear with that next shot of heroin. In recognition of this, street addicts will point out that their motivation for using drugs often changes after they become addicted. Whereas prior to addiction, they used drugs to get "high," they now must first "feed their habits" (i.e., avoid withdrawal) and then, if there are any drugs left over, get high.

Heroin is generally considered by most persons, including many drug experts, as being an extremely dangerous drug. In fact, it is often viewed as the hardest of the "hard" drugs. Unfortunately, this stereotype is only partially accurate. Heroin is a physiologically addicting substance. Within a relatively short period of time, regular use (three times daily over the period of several weeks) will lead to addiction. Further, the heroin user always runs the risk of death due to overdose. (There are some observers who believe that the cause of overdose in many cases is allergic reaction to the diluents such as quinine or lactose, which are used to "cut" the drug, rather than to the actual physiological effects of the heroin itself.) It is also true that addicts in general suffer from a large number of other diseases. In the popular mind these diseases are the result of heroin use, while the truth is that these diseases result from the use of unclean needles rather than from the heroin. For instance, addicts contract AIDS by sharing needles contaminated by other users whose blood is positive for the AIDS virus. Hepatitis and other diseases are contracted in the same way. As we shall see, the street addict lifestyle, which is so consumed with the search for drugs and the money needed to pay for them, is a physically demanding and dangerous enterprise. Addicts typically have poor diets and poor health care habits and are always subject to the dangers and violence of the street. Thus, it is not surprising that persons associate heroin with misery and death.

Medical researchers, however, are hard put to find serious ill effects which can be attributed directly to the heroin. Other than the real risk of physical addiction and the somewhat nominal risk of overdose, few chronic physiological effects have been found in addicts. In reviewing the available studies, Hofmann (1975: 84) concludes:

> Thus far, numerous searches for possible functional or structural abnormalities resulting from the chronic use of heroin, which could be attributed to some effect of the drug itself, have proved fruitless; even when the drug has been used regularly for a number of years, no marked functional disturbances have been detected during life, and findings on autopsy have been essentially negative."

The Importance of the Three S's

In a recent publication (Stephens, 1987), I emphasized the importance of the three "S's" in understanding why people use drugs. These are the substance, the set, and the setting. I have already discussed substance. Different types of drugs impart different kinds of highs. Heroin highs are often said to be almost sexually orgasmic. Indeed the heroin high is described as being twofold.

Upon injection there is the intense "rush" which is dramatic and short-lived and is followed by a semi-somnolent state known as the "nod." The "nod" lasts longer and in it the addict feels a sense of overall well-being. Contrast this high with that of barbiturates where the euphoric feeling is akin to being drunk on alcohol. Thus, the substance is important in understanding why someone takes a certain drug.

The second "S" is equally important. This is the set, or user's expectation of what the effect of the drug will be. If users expect certain reactions from a drug, then that reaction will usually occur. In fact, persons can experience effects even when they have not actually taken a drug. This is the so-called placebo effect. (For a review of placebo effects, see Leavitt [1982].)

The final "S" and the principal focus of this book is the setting. Typically, setting has referred to the immediate environment in which the drug is taken. Classic research by Becker (1963), for instance, shows that a person's reaction to LSD can be accounted for by the setting in which the person takes the drug. If others in the setting define the experience as pleasurable, then the "trip" is pleasurable. If there is no "guide" to interpret the experience, it is more likely that the individual will have a "bad trip." While, as we shall see in Chapter 4, immediate setting is crucial to understanding beginning and continued heroin use, I want to expand the concept to include the larger sociocultural setting in which the drugs are used. One major theme of this book is that setting, defined in this way, is crucial to understanding why people become and remain addicted to heroin.

Psychoactive Drug Use in the United States

What do we know about drug use in this larger social setting? Fortunately, epidemiological data are available which allow us to estimate prevalence rates for the use of various psychoactive substances. Table 1 contains data on the prevalence of drug use from a series of national household surveys of drug use conducted for the National Institute on Drug Abuse. The samples for these studies are selected to be as representative a sample of the

American population as possible. A number of interesting figures are contained in Table 1, which is an estimate for each year of the total percentage of persons who *ever* used the indicated substance, except as prescribed by a physician.

First, as one can see, the substances which have been used by the greatest percentage of people are alcohol, cigarettes, marihuana, and to a lesser extent cocaine and some psychotherapeutic substances. Except for the first three of these substances, the vast majority of Americans report that they have never used any psychoactive substances. Note also that for almost all substances in almost all age groups, there is a steady decline in use since 1979. (This very interesting statistic seriously questions the idea that America is in the grip of a drug epidemic; however, that is another story. See Stephens [1990].)

Of most immediate concern to us here is the extent of heroin use in the population. As one can see, recent studies indicate that approximately 2 percent or less of youth and young adults and 2.1 percent or less of older adults report that they have ever used heroin. Thus, heroin use is not a widespread phenomenon in American society.

Table 2 displays data on recency of psychoactive drug use. Specifically, it contains the percentage of persons who report that they have used the indicated psychoactive substance in the month before they were interviewed. As one would expect, the figures decline markedly from those observed in Table 1. Moreover, the pattern observed in Table 1 is repeated here; there has been a dramatic decline in usage since 1979. Note, too, that heroin use is extremely low. For years in which the data are available, usage rates are less than 0.5 percent. Thus, recent heroin use is found for only a small portion of American society.

Who are these heroin users? Table 3 presents a partial answer to this question. It presents data from the 1985 National Institute on Drug Abuse (N.I.D.A.) household survey. These are the most recent detailed published figures. As one can see, heroin use is not randomly distributed throughout the American population. It is a phenomenon found among older youth and young adults, males, and minority groups (except for 26–34-year-old whites whose heroin use rates are higher than for the other two ethnic groups). It is associated more with metropolitan areas although it is fairly

TABLE 1
LIFETIME PREVALENCE OF DRUG USE FOR SELECTED YEARS BY DRUG CATEGORY (PERCENTAGES)

	YOUTH (12–17)					YOUNG ADULTS (18–25)					(26+)		OLDER ADULTS (26–34)			(35+)		
	1974	1979	1982	1985	1988	1974	1979	1982	1985	1988	1974	1979	1982	1985	1988	1982	1985	1988
Marijuana	23.0	30.9	26.7	23.6	17.4	52.7	68.2	64.1	60.3	62.1	9.9	19.6	55.7	58.5	62.1	11.7	15.9	19.6
Hallucinogens	6.0	7.1	5.2	3.3	3.5	16.6	25.1	21.1	11.3	17.7	1.3	4.5	19.2	16.9	17.7	2.0	2.4	2.7
Cocaine	3.6	5.4	6.5	4.9	3.4	12.7	27.5	28.3	25.2	26.5	0.9	4.3	21.7	24.1	26.5	4.0	4.2	4.0
Heroin	1.0	0.5	*	*	0.6	4.5	3.5	1.2	1.2	2.1	0.5	1.0	3.5	2.6	2.1	*	0.5	0.8
Stimulants	5.0	3.4	6.7	5.6	4.2	17.0	18.2	18.0	17.1	15.4	3.0	5.8	15.2	18.3	15.4	3.0	4.2	3.6
Sedatives	5.0	3.2	5.8	4.1	2.4	15.0	17.0	18.7	11.0	7.9	2.0	3.5	13.0	12.4	7.9	2.0	2.6	1.7
Tranquilizers	3.0	4.1	4.9	4.8	2.0	10.0	15.8	15.1	12.0	9.3	2.0	3.1	9.8	13.9	9.3	1.4	4.7	2.9
Analgesics	—	3.2	4.2	5.8	4.2	—	11.8	12.1	11.3	9.7	—	2.7	8.6	13.3	9.7	1.4	2.8	2.6
Any non-medical use of psychotherapeutics	—	7.3	10.3	12.1	7.7	—	29.5	28.4	26.0	22.1	—	9.2	21.1	27.2	22.1	4.5	9.0	7.5
Alcohol	54.0	70.3	65.2	55.5	50.2	81.6	95.3	94.6	92.6	93.3	73.2	72.4	95.8	93.1	93.3	85.6	88.0	87.0
Cigarettes	52.0	54.1	49.5	45.2	42.3	68.8	82.8	76.9	75.6	80.8	65.4	39.7	85.4	80.7	80.8	76.3	80.4	79.3

* Less than ½ of 1 percent. Defined as illegal use of stimulants, sedatives, tranquilizers, or analgesics.
— Estimate not available.

Sources: National Household Survey on Drug Abuse: Population Estimate, 1988 (NIDA, 1989c).
National Household Survey on Drug Abuse: Main Findings, 1985 (NIDA, 1986).

TABLE 2
PERSONS WHO USED IN PAST MONTH – FOR SELECTED YEARS BY DRUG CATEGORY (PERCENTAGES)

	YOUTH (12–17)					YOUNG ADULTS (18–25)					OLDER ADULTS							
											(26+)		(26–34)			(35+)		
	1974	1979	1982	1985	1988	1974	1979	1982	1985	1988	1974	1979	1982	1985	1988	1982	1985	1988
Marijuana	12.0	16.7	11.5	12.0	6.4	25.2	35.4	27.4	21.8	15.5	2.0	6.0	16.9	16.9	10.8	3.0	2.3	
Hallucinogens	1.3	2.2	1.4	1.2	0.8	2.5	4.4	1.7	1.9	1.9	*	*	*	1.5	*	*	*	
Cocaine	1.0	1.4	1.6	1.5	1.1	3.1	9.3	6.8	7.6	4.5	*	0.9	3.3	6.1	2.6	0.5	0.5	
Heroin	*	*	*	*	*	*	*	*	*	*	*	*	*	*	*	*	*	
Stimulants	1.0	1.2	2.6	1.6	1.2	3.7	3.5	4.7	3.7	2.4	*	0.5	1.8	2.2	0.9	*	*	
Sedatives	1.0	1.1	1.3	1.0	0.6	1.6	2.8	2.6	1.6	0.9	*	*	1.3	1.2	0.6	*	*	
Tranquilizers	1.0	0.6	0.9	0.6	0.2	1.2	2.1	1.6	1.6	1.0	*	*	1.0	1.7	1.2	*	0.8	
Analgesics	—	0.6	0.7	1.6	0.9	—	1.0	1.0	1.8	1.5	—	*	1.3	2.2	0.9	*	*	
Any non-medical use of psychotherapeutics	—	2.3	3.8	3.0	2.4	—	6.2	7.0	6.3	3.8	—	1.1	4.2	5.3	2.7	*	1.5	
Alcohol	34.0	37.2	30.2	31.0	25.2	69.3	75.9	70.9	71.4	65.3	54.5	61.3	73.0	70.0	64.2	55.2		
Cigarettes	25.0	12.1	14.7	15.3	11.8	48.8	42.6	39.5	36.8	35.2	39.1	36.9	43.9	40.3	37.1	31.4		

* Less than ½ of 1 percent. Defined as illegal use of stimulants, sedatives, tranquilizers, or analgesics.
— Estimate not available
Sources: National Household Survey on Drug Abuse: Population Estimate, 1988 (NIDA, 1989c).
National Household Survey on Drug Abuse: Main Findings, 1985 (NIDA, 1986).

TABLE 3

PERCENT REPORTING HEROIN USE IN LIFETIME BY AGE GROUP AND
DEMOGRAPHIC CHARACTERISTICS: 1985

DEMOGRAPHIC CHARACTERISTIC	AGE GROUP (YEARS)				
	12–17	18–25	26–34	35+	TOTAL
Total	*	1.2	2.6	0.5	1.0
Sex					
Male	*	1.6	3.6	1.0	1.6
Female	*	0.7	1.5	*	0.5
Race/Ethnicity					
White	*	1.1	2.8	*	1.0
Black	*	1.5	1.6	1.6	1.4
Hispanic	*	1.4	2.1	*	0.8
Population Density					
Large Metro	*	2.2	2.4	*	1.2
Small Metro	*	0.6	2.7	1.0	1.1
Nonmetro	*	1.3	2.4	*	0.8
Region					
Northeast	*	1.1	2.3	0.8	1.1
North Central	*	0.7	2.4	0.7	1.0
South	0.7	1.8	2.9	*	1.1
West	*	0.8	2.6	*	0.8
Adult Education					
Less than high school	N/A	3.8	3.1	*	1.1
High school graduate	N/A	0.9	2.1	*	0.9
Some college	N/A	*	4.4	0.5	1.4
College graduate	N/A	*	1.3	1.2	1.1
Current Employment					
Full-time	0.7	0.7	2.2	1.0	1.2
Part-time	*	1.5	3.9	*	1.0
Unemployed	*	2.2	7.6	*	2.3
Other	*	1.6	1.6	*	0.5

* Less than ½ of 1 percent.

Source: NIDA, National Household Survey on Drug Abuse, 1988.

evenly distributed throughout the various regions of the country. Heroin users are much more likely to be unemployed or employed only part-time and to have relatively low levels of educational attainment (except for those 26--34 years old.) In general, it would appear that the composite picture of the heroin user that emerges from these data is of a young, male, minority group member who resides in a metropolitan area and is often likely to be underemployed and educationally disadvantaged.

Table 4 contains another set of data which help us to describe the nature of heroin addiction in the United States. These data are drawn from the Drug Abuse Warning Network (DAWN) project sponsored by N.I.D.A. This project monitors drug related emergency room admissions and drug-related deaths as reported by medical examiners. From the total list of drugs (including many non-psychoactive substances such as aspirin), I selected notable "street drugs" which also happen to be the most frequently mentioned psychoactive substances. A single admission can account for more than one mention if the person had used more than one drug. The data in Table 4 report on drug related admissions to 738 hospitals located primarily in twenty-one metropolitan areas. As one can see for the listed drugs, the greatest number of emergency room mentions was for cocaine, followed by alcohol in combination with some other drug. Heroin was third with 19,370 mentions. Of the total number of mentions, Blacks accounted for half and Hispanics for about 16 percent. For cocaine, blacks accounted for 61 percent and Hispanics about 10 percent. Indeed, save for methamphetamine, all of these drugs are disproportionately mentioned for minorities.

Table 5 contains the final set of data regarding ethnicity and use of street drugs. It contains DAWN autopsy reports from 87 medical examiners on what drugs were implicated in the deaths. The results are somewhat different from those reported in Table 4. Yet at the same time they support similar conclusions. Except for those due to PCP and cocaine, drug abuse related deaths are higher among whites than Blacks or Hispanics. Yet drug abuse deaths overall are disproportionately found among minorities. While blacks constitute 12 percent of the American population and Hispanics comprise 8 percent of the population, they account for 35 percent and 18 percent respectively of the heroin-related deaths. For cocaine-related deaths, the rates are 45 and 17 percent respectively.

Overall, these data indicate that heroin use and use of other street drugs, by and large, is concentrated in urban areas generally among younger persons who are economically and educationally disadvantaged. If one considers emergency room admissions and medical examiner reports to be indicators of serious drug abuse problems, then it would appear that, while the evidence is somewhat fuzzy, the extent of such problems is generally more widespread among minority populations.

TABLE 4
PERCENTAGE OF EMERGENCY ROOM MENTIONS
BY TYPE OF DRUG AND ETHNICITY
DAWN DATA — 1988

	WHITE	BLACK	HISPANIC	OTHER	TOTAL
Cocaine	28.9	61.2	9.5	.01	100.0 (57,626)
Alcohol in Combination	48.4	40.5	10.1	0.9	99.9 (42,764)
Heroin	33.3	50.5	15.6	0.5	99.9 (19,370)
Marijuana	43.5	47.0	8.7	.01	100.0 (9,979)
PCP	24.5	61.2	13.8	0.5	100.0 (7,874)
Methamphetamine	83.8	7.5	6.9	1.8	100.0 (2,757)

TABLE 5
PERCENT DISTRIBUTION OF DRUG RELATED DEATHS
BY DRUG AND ETHNICITY

DRUG	WHITE	BLACK	HISPANIC	OTHER	TOTAL
Heroin	45.9	35.0	18.3	0.8	100.0 (2,232)
Methamphetamine	80.7	8.0	9.3	2.0	100.0 (150)
PCP	29.3	52.5	17.1	1.1	100.0 (181)
Alcohol in Combination	49.8	32.0	17.9	0.3	100.0 (2,349)
Marijuana	61.4	29.0	9.7	—	100.1 (259)
Cocaine	37.3	45.1	17.1	0.5	100.0 (3,022)

Source: NIDA, Data from the Drug Abuse Warning Network (DAWN), 1989.

Outline of this Book

Having considered some needed background information, we are now ready to embark on that journey promised earlier in this chapter. Chapter 2 will provide an overview of symbolic interactionist and role theories—the theoretical perspectives underlying the present theory. Chapter 3 will develop the hypothesis-based theory and cite the relevant sociocultural and other literature which supports the hypotheses. Chapter 4 will describe the street scene in all its richness, portray the processes in becoming and being a street addict, and provide yet further support for the hypotheses presented in Chapter 3. Chapter 5 will analyze, from both structural and historical perspectives, the origins of the street addict role. Chapter 6 will examine and critique the individualistic physiologically and psychologically based theories which dominate the field of drug abuse today. Chapter 7 will provide a review and critique, from the sociocultural perspective, of the major modalities used to treat narcotics addicts today. The book concludes in Chapter 8 with a discussion of the various proposals for dealing with the "drug problem" in America, including a set of recommendations which emerge from a socioculturally informed perspective.

Chapter Two

The Symbolic Interactionist Perspective

One of the major paradigms within the general field of sociology (Turner, 1974) is what Blumer has termed "symbolic interactionism." The founding father of the symbolic interactionist approach is George Herbert Mead, who outlined the theory in *Mind, Self and Society* (1934). Since Mead's time, a number of other theorists (Linton, 1936; Strauss, 1959; Goffman, 1959; Blumer, 1969; Turner, 1978; and Stryker, 1980 among others) have expanded the perspective.

In its simplest form, symbolic interaction theory asserts that persons interact with others utilizing both verbal and nonverbal symbols.[1] Symbolic interactionists place special emphasis on language as the most important symbol used by persons in their interactions. It is through symbolic interaction with others that a person develops the self. The self is basically derived from interacting with others, having them react to the actor's actions, and thus shaping the actor's view of self. All of these "others" do not have equal influence in shaping the self; some are more important and are seen as "significant others." Symbolic interactionists have also recognized that interactions between persons do not usually occur in a random fashion but rather are structured and based on expectations of how certain actors will, in fact, act. These structured behavioral expectations are called "roles." Roles, in turn, are attached to social positions and are arranged (usually in some sort of socially determined hierarchy) in the social structure.

It has also been recognized that not all self-concepts are equally valued by the actor. Rather 'selves' or 'identities' have differential salience to the actor and can be arranged in an identity hierarchy.

There are many determinants of which self-concepts will be valued more than others.

The preceding is an oversimplified version of the basic symbolic interactionist approach. My purpose is not to explicate fully symbolic interactionist theory; this task has been accomplished in several published works (Stryker, 1980; Hewitt, 1984; Heiss, 1981; Petras and Metzer, 1975). Rather, in this chapter I shall attempt to describe the chief concepts (and related controversies) of symbolic interactionist theory. It is with these conceptual building blocks that I construct my own theory of heroin use, which appears in the next chapter.

Principal Terms of Symbolic Interaction Theory

Self

For all symbolic interactionists, clearly the most important concept is that of the self. The self has two components: object and process. It is basically both an answer to the question "Who am I?" (the object) and the internal process by which the answer to the question is derived (the process) (Hewitt, 1984: 89–91). A major contribution of symbolic interactionism is found in the theoretically important statement that the self can become an object to itself. Through the use of language, actors can attach names to others and to themselves and their actions. Hewitt notes that

> As individuals engage in social activity, then, each can represent that activity within his own mind, and act according to how he thinks others will act. Indeed, not only does the individual represent the activities of the group as a whole and imagine various scenarios taking place, but he also interacts with himself. This can be accomplished because the act of giving himself the name that others gave him also has the result of constituting the individual as an object in his own world. The individual does not merely represent a world of social objects—

people—of which he is a part, but he acts toward (and interacts with) those objects including himself. (Hewitt, 1984: 71)

The Self as Process

Because of the formulation of self as process, several conceptual problems have been presented to symbolic interactionists. One such issue is the degree to which self is determined by others vs. how much it is constructed by the actor.

Basically, the question is: "Is the self too socially structured, too overdetermined by the actions of others?" (Wrong, 1961) Symbolic interactionists, along with many other social scientists and philosophers, have long been plagued by this question. Mead seems to have attempted an answer by describing two aspects of the self. The first is the 'I' which emphasizes the "immediate, spontaneous and impulsive aspect of conduct" (Hewitt, 1984: 72). According to Mead, the 'I' gives the sense of freedom and of initiative. (Mead, 1934: 177). The 'Me' on the other hand, is more of the socially derived and, to some extent, socially determined self. Through many social interactions the actor derives a socially based self-conception (the 'Me'). In many ways, then, the self is a product of the constant internal dialogue between the 'I' and the 'Me'. It is because of this dialogue that some symbolic interactionists insist the self is a process and not a structure (Hewitt, 1984: 71–75).

Despite Mead's attempt, this issue of the social "determinedness" of the self remains a concern in more recent versions of symbolic interaction theory. In fact, various camps of symbolic interactionism seem to be arrayed along a continuum defined by this issue. Nearer one end of the continuum is labelling theory (see Lemert, 1951), which portrays a rather passive individual who is a recipient of the self-definition attached to him by the society. Closer to the other end of the continuum is Blumer's brand of symbolic interactionism, which stresses the tentative and emergent nature of the interaction situation. This perspective portrays the actor as much more of a master of his or her fate and a creator of his or her self through interaction. Somewhere in between are found theorists like McCall and Simmons (1978) with their role identity model and Goffman (1959) with his dramaturgical approach. Both of these latter approaches seem to emphasize not only that persons express their desired selves in interaction situations but that the self concept is also shaped by interaction with others, making the self a creation of both the actor and others.

This raises another closely related theoretical point, namely, the changeability (or conversely the stability) of the self. All symbolic interactionists are committed to the viewpoint that self can change. However, they seem to differ somewhat on how much and how quickly the self can change. Indeed, this issue also seems to define an additional continuum along which symbolic interactionists can be arrayed. The role theorists seem to be committed to a more enduring self whereas Blumer (1969), for example, seems almost to portray a self in the process of continual change.

Perhaps Hewitt (1984) has made the best attempt to resolve these issues when he discusses the nature of personhood. He says:

> Three fundamental ideas will guide our discussion of the nature of the person.
>
> First, the self has a dual location, for people are the objects both of their own acts and of the acts of others. In other words, the self is not merely something the person creates, but also is something created for the person by others.
>
> Second, persons are objects (to themselves and others) in two different respects. The self is a situated object—in each situation, the person constitutes himself or herself as an object by taking the role of others in that situation. The self is also a biographical object—that is, persons constitute themselves as objects by reflecting on their life experiences as a whole.
>
> Third, we can analytically divide persons into three aspects: Their location in relation to one another, their qualities and attributes insofar as these enter into their images of one another and themselves, and their evaluations of themselves and one another. (Hewitt, 1984: 106)

Basically then, Hewitt is saying that the self in interaction can be an object both to others and to the actor. Persons are also known (both to themselves and others) in concrete situations (usually associated with situated roles) and as individuals who have more cumulative and more enduring biographically rooted self-concepts. Accordingly, persons can be socially located in terms of how they will behave in specific instances. As Hewitt points out, husbands and wives have cognitive maps which socially locate each other in terms of particular behavioral expectations (breadwinner, sexual partner, housekeeper, etc.). In addition, persons have more enduring qualities which are both social objects and objects to self. (For instance, husbands and wives think of themselves as loving or abusive, etc.) Persons also appraise one another in evaluative terms such as good or bad, etc. Important to this evaluation is self-esteem, which is the product of both the person's own and other's evaluation of the person's sense of worth.

The Self as Object

As I have said, self is also an object. There are four content areas of the self:[2] an identity set, a set of qualities, a set of evaluations, and a set of self-confidence levels (Heiss 1981). The identity set consists of positional levels which state where one fits in the social world. (This is primarily a statement of one's roles.) Secondly, adjectives are used to refer to the qualities of the self-concept (such as tall, thin, and other socially recognized categories.) Thirdly, there are self-evaluations which are, according to Heiss (1981), adjectives which are attached to the identities and qualities of the self-concept. Finally, there is the person's level of self-confidence, which refers to "the person's estimate of the extent to which he or she can master challenges and overcome obstacles, that is, the extent to which things can be made to turn out as wanted" (Heiss, 1981: 59).

In the final analysis, then, the self is both a complicated process and object which is both enduring and changing. "The person is thus a complex reality—an enduring object as well as one constituted from moment to moment, an object of his or her own acts and those of others, an object involved in social relationships, with attributed characteristics and with a sense of worth. To introduce order into this reality, we must pay attention particularly to the relationships between the situated and biographical aspects of the person" (Hewitt, 1984: 114).

Role

The other chief concept in most interactionist theories, and the most important variable in the present theory of heroin use, is that of 'role.' As with the concept of self, role has been defined in different ways. Some theorists, such as Biddle (1979), define it simply as patterned human behavior. However, others, such as Heiss (1981) prefer to think of roles as expectations. He says:

> I believe that role should be, in a literal sense, the central variable in any role theory. All role theories should account for roles and also use roles as key factors in the explanation of other phenomena. From this point of view it is preferable to define roles as expectations rather than as behavior. The ultimate dependent variable in social psychological theory is social behavior, and if roles refer to actual behavior there would be little for roles to explain. (Heiss, 1981: 95)

I agree with what Heiss says in the above passage. The definition of role used in my theory is that of "behavioral expectations for the occupant of the role." As Heiss points out, one must then address the question of whose expectations are the most relevant— those of society, certain others', or the actor's? I would agree, although hesitantly, with Heiss that we must ultimately define expectations from the actor's viewpoint.[3] In dyadic interaction, for example, both persons, as members of a role set (see Merton, 1957), bring their own expectations into the interaction. These expectations are based on the roles which are appropriate to the interaction. Usually, there is a fair degree of predictability about how each of the individuals will interact, because they share common agreement on what constitutes appropriate behavior in this role set. Sometimes, however, there is disagreement on what is appropriate role behavior. In this case, to understand the actor's behavior, we must understand the actor's definition of the situation. My hesitancy in focusing on the actor's perspective is due to the fact that somehow defining expectations in such a way is nearly tautological, and comes very close to being untestable. However, from an analytical point of view, the concept need not be inherently untestable nor tautological.

As with the concept of self, various theorists disagree on the nature of roles, specifically on how tightly structured they are and to what extent they dictate the actor's behavior. This difference underlies the debate between the structuralist and interactionist positions.[4] The structuralists (such as Gross, et al., [1958]) see roles as being fairly tightly defined "blueprints for action." The interactionists see roles as much less determined and structured. McCall and Simmons, the two leading interactionists, agree that "the expectations that comprise a 'social role' in this sense are entirely too vague, incomplete and poorly specified in most instances to serve as genuine guides to action" (McCall and Simmons, 1978: 64).

In my view, part of the debate between structuralist and interactionist is dependent upon what the theorist is attempting to predict. Some interactionist theory (see especially McCall and Simmons [1978]) attempts to understand the behavior of individual actors in specific situations. In other words, it seems to ask the question, "Why does the person act in certain ways in specific interactions with others?" Thus, the spotlight is on the processes used by the individual actor in a designated interaction situation. There is much emphasis on exchange, negotiation, and the fluid nature of the self in the myriad of interaction situations with which the individual person is confronted.

The structuralist position, and the one I will utilize in the development of the present theory of heroin use, argues that the goal is not solely to understand interaction processes but rather to understand the general and regularly predictable behavior of a group of individuals defined by their roles. I believe that we can generally predict the behaviors of a group of individuals over time given a knowledge of their roles. Using a statistical analogy, we can explain a significant amount—but certainly not all—of the variance if we know the role (or roles) of the individual.[5] For instance, knowing that a person is a professor will allow us to predict much about that person's behavior, past history of behaviors, and even many of his or her attitudes. But, as I have said, it will not predict all of the behavior. The professor may be an interesting or boring lecturer, a competent or less than competent scholar, and so forth. Any residual variance remains to be explained by the concept of the self. In the final analysis, I agree with Heiss's "moderate" view of roles which "suggests that except when we find ourselves in new and unfamiliar situations, roles learned in previous interactions provide us with general guides to proper behavior" (Heiss, 1981: 67).[6]

While I think that the interactionist model posited by McCall and Simmons (1978) overemphasizes the indeterminacy of roles, they have nevertheless developed an important role-oriented (and self-oriented) concept. This is "role-identity," which they define as the imaginative view of the self as one likes to think of one's self in being and acting as an occupant of a role (McCall and Simmons, 1978: 65).

> Each role-identity of each individual thus has two aspects, the conventional and the idiosyncratic. The relative proportion of these two aspects varies from person to person, and from identity to identity for the same individual. Some people add little to the role-expectations they have learned; others modify and elaborate culturally defined roles to such extreme extents that the roles become unrecognizable to other people and the individuals are regarded as eccentric or mentally ill. Most of us, fortunately, fall somewhere between. (McCall and Simmons, 1978: 68)

Not all role-identities are of equal importance to the actor. The salience of a role-identity (or probability that it will be invoked in a given situation) is the result of five factors: (1) its prominence (the importance of the role-identity vis-à-vis other role-identities to the person); (2) the degree of support by others for the role-identity (that is, social support for one's identity); the person's need or desire for the kinds and amounts of (3) intrinsic and (4) extrinsic gratification (or rewards) ordinarily gained through its performance; and (5) the perceived degree of opportunity for its profitable enactment in given circumstances (McCall and Simmons, 1978). Thus, all identities are not equally important to the person, but rather are arranged in a salience hierarchy where the ones which are more valued are more likely to be enacted.

Commitment

All roles (and self-concepts) differ in the degree of commitment the actor has to them. Commitment is "the degree to which the individual has committed himself to the particular contents of this role-identity, has gambled his regard for himself on living up to certain imaginations of self. If, for example, he has staked much of his self-esteem on becoming a recognized sculptor, that identity will loom prominently in his self-organization" (McCall and Simmons, 1978: 75).

Stryker and Serpe define commitment as "the degree to which the person's relationships to specified sets of others depends on his or her being a particular kind of person, i.e. occupying a particular position in an organized structure of relationships and playing a particular role" (Stryker and Serpe, 1982: 207). Stryker suggests:

To the degree that one's relationships to specified sets of other persons depend on being a particular kind of person, one is committed to being that kind of person. If the maintenance of ties to a set of others is important to the person, and dependent upon being—say—a member of a sorority that person is committed to being a member of a sorority. Since entering into social relationships is premised on the attribution and acceptance of positions and associated roles, then commitments are premised on identities. (Stryker, 1980: 61--62)

In the theory to be presented here, the concept of commitment is central. It connotes the amount of investment a person has made in both the self-concept and interactions with selected types of significant others when he or she assumes a certain role. Those roles and self-concepts or role identities to which the person are most committed are at the top of the identity salience hierarchy.

Some Additional Role Theory Terms

Role theory has developed a number of other concepts which will be useful to the explanation of heroin use. There are 'role merger,' 'role conflict,' 'role strain,' and 'reference groups.' In addition, a review of the basic sociological concepts of social structure, culture, and socialization will be helpful.

Role Merger

Turner (1978) says that the merger of role with person occurs when attitudes and behavior developed as an expression of one role carried over into other situations. That is, role merger occurs when a particular role becomes so much a part of a person's identity (i.e., ranks consistently higher than other roles on a salience hierarchy) that he or she uses it in a wide variety of situations. Role merger is found most notably when a role is employed in such a wide variety of situations that it is invoked even in situations where it might seem to others to be inappropriate.

The concept of 'role engulfment,' developed by Schur (1971) to understand deviant behavior, is very similar to that of role merger. For the deviant, "role engulfment occurs when he or she is caught up in a deviant role, to find that it has become highly salient in his overall personal identity (or concept of self), that his behavior is increasingly organized around the role, and that cultural expectations attached to the role have come to have precedence, or increased salience relative to other expectations, in the organization of his activities and general way of life" (Schur, 1971: 69).

Also closely related to the concepts of role engulfment and role merger is the concept of 'master status.' Borrowing from Hughes (1945), Becker (1963) argues that some statuses in our society override all other statuses and acquire a certain priority. The role of deviant has this type of master status:

One receives the status as a result of breaking a rule and the identification proves to be more important than most others. One will be identified as a deviant first, before other identifications are made. The question is raised: "What kind of person would break such an important rule?" And the answer is given: "One who is different from the rest of us, who cannot or will not act as a moral human being and therefore might break other important rules." The deviant identification becomes the controlling one. (Becker, 1963: 35)

Because of this reaction by others towards the deviant (this labelling process is discussed later in this chapter), the person is very likely to integrate this deviant identity and its attendant status into his or her self-concept.

Role Conflict

When an individual experiences behavioral expectations which are inconsistent, the person experiences role conflict.

Role conflict exists when there are contradictory expectations that attach to some position in a social relationship. Such expectations may call for incompatible performances; they may require that one hold two norms or values which logically call for opposing behaviors; or they may demand that one role necessitates the expenditure of time and energy such that it is difficult or even impossible to carry out the obligations of another role. (Stryker, 1980: 73)

Thus, role conflict can arise among the competing expectations for a single role (intra-role conflict), or it may develop out of the competing and simultaneous demands of several roles (inter-role conflict). In the intra-role conflict, the role may demand conflicting and possibly opposing behaviors. An example might be a chairperson of an academic department. Such an individual is considered both a faculty member and peer and yet at the same time may be expected to perform nonegalitarian administrative functions (such as determining teaching loads and annual pay increases.) Inter-role conflict is seen when the demands of two different roles are inconsistent (as in the case when a woman feels conflict between her career and her role as a mother). Role conflict has potential negative implications for the person, yet it is also a fertile ground for the individual's creative potential. (For more extensive discussions of role conflict, see VanSell, Brief and Schuler [1981] and Stryker and Macke [1978].)

Role Strain

Another important role oriented concept is role strain. According to Goode (1960), role strain is a felt difficulty in enacting the requirements of a role. The sources of role strain can be many, including the physical, psychological, or emotional inability of the person to play (or continue to play) a particular role. A person may simply have committed his or her self either to the expected enactment of too many roles or to roles for which he or she is not equipped in some physical, emotional, or other way. Whatever the reason, when a person feels that it is difficult or impossible to enact a role (as expected by others), that individual is said to experience role strain.

Reference Groups

Reference groups are "those social groups that provide generalized others to whom the individual refers his or her conduct and against whose standards that conduct is evaluated, [and] may include groups of which one is not an actual member as well as groups to which one belongs" (Hewitt, 1984: 84). Reference groups are very important to the actor as they provide, among other things, socialization into roles, motivation for assuming certain roles, and feedback as to how adequately the actor is enacting the role. Given the fact that each of us has many reference groups, all such groups are not of equal value. Symbolic interactionists label those reference groups most important to us as "significant others."

Persons stand in relationship to others in the reference group primarily through what are called "role sets." Role sets are "the complement of role relationships which persons have by virtue of occupying a particular social status" (i.e., a position in a social structure) (Merton, 1957: 369). In essence then, role sets are the expectations held by both ego and other around a specific role.

Social Structure

The symbolic interactionists have been criticized by some as being astructural, that is, unconcerned with social structure, which many sociological theorists believe to be of central concern. I agree with some symbolic interactionists (see particularly Hewitt [1984], Stryker [1980], and Maines [1977]) that this criticism is generally unwarranted. While it is true that symbolic interactionists have focused on interaction at the micro-social level, they nevertheless have provided the crucial concept of role as the fundamental bridge between the individual and the social structure. In fact, according to the symbolic interactionists, roles are the building blocks of social structure. Basically, the argument they propose is as follows. Roles, or behavioral expectations between persons, are clustered into role sets. Role sets, in turn, are organized around certain functions in the society (such as the religious, economic, familial and other functions). These clusters of role sets are called institutions and in fact constitute what macro-theorists recognize as the social structure of a society. Gerth and Mills (1953), in their classic *Character and Social Structure*, point to the major importance of role as the link between character structure (which includes the characteristics of man as a biological and psychic being and as a player of roles) and social structure (the institutions of the society).

An important aspect of social structure is that roles and role-sets are arranged not only according to function (as in Gerth and Mills's 1953 institutional order), but also in terms of the prestige accorded to a particular role. Usually the society demonstrates this prestige by allocating both symbolic (deference) and tangible rewards (money and other scarce resources) to those roles (and role occupants) further up in the status hierarchy. That is, the status of a role (and role player) is determined by hierarchical position or location in the social structure.

Symbolic interactionists also realize that access to various roles is not equal among all persons in the society. Either because of the person's own qualities and abilities or the requirements (or prejudices) of the society, some persons are not allowed to play certain roles. That is, some persons can never achieve certain roles, because they are blocked from doing so either by their own limitations or by the entrance rules imposed by the social structure.

Culture

Despite the importance of the concept of 'culture,' symbolic inter-actionists have not accorded it a central place in their theory.[7] For purposes of the theory developed here, culture is defined as the sum total of language, roles, statuses, norms, and values of the society. (The physical artifacts of the society, of less interest to symbolic interactionism, could be labelled as physical culture.) Of particular importance to a symbolic interactionist definition of culture, I would argue, is the central place that language holds. It is primarily through language that a culture is transmitted between persons and across time.

Sociologists in general, and symbolic interactionists in particular (see, for instance, Lemert [1951]), have recognized that in heterogeneous, industrialized societies there are actually many groups which do not share all of the values of the larger society. These groups have sets of values which may be different from, indeed, at times opposed to the values of the larger societies.[8] Such sets of different values, norms, and roles are called "subcultures." Thus, these subcultures provide for their participants reference groups (including most particularly significant others) and role expectations which dictate that certain behaviors—possibly defined as deviant by the larger society—are considered normal and expected in the subculture.

Socialization

The culture (or subculture) is transmitted from one person to another both within and between generations. How is this cultural transmission accomplished? Through socialization, or the learning of the culture through symbolic interaction, one comes to learn the norms and values of one's society.[9] The symbolic interactionists, as contrasted to many schools of psychology, emphasize the point that socialization is a lifelong process. As Brim (1966) notes, socialization received in childhood cannot be fully adequate as preparation for the tasks demanded of him or her in adulthood, such as occupational roles. Brim argues that adult socialization basically entails a shift in content from a concern with values and motives (achieved in childhood) to a concern with overt behavior.

> The usual objective of socialization in the later-life stages is to get one to practice a new combination of skills already acquired, to combine existing elements into new forms, to trim and polish existing material, rather than to learn wholly new complexes or responses, as in the case of the relatively untrained child, for whom the socialization effort starts with little more than initial intelligence and primary drives. (Brim, 1966: 28)

Other sociologists maintain that adult socialization can involve a total transformation of the self, rather than mere refinements and adjustments. While I agree with Brim that for most persons adult socialization processes are as he describes, I feel that more enduring concepts of self (the biographical self) are also capable of relatively profound changes. This is especially true in cases where there is a confluence of role merger, labelling and degradation processes. (This point will be dealt with in greater detail in the coming theory of heroin use.)

Socialization, while usually occurring through interaction with others, can also occur in relative isolation. The person need not interact directly with those who play a role to which the actor aspires. A person can signify to himself the requirements of a role. We say that such a person has engaged in anticipatory socialization.

The Symbolic Interactionist Perspective in Deviance Theory

Inasmuch as heroin addiction is considered by the larger American society to be a very deviant behavior, it might be fruitful to see how the symbolic interactionalist perspective has been applied by others to the study of deviant behavior.

Labelling Theory

A number of sociologists, heavily influenced by Meadian thought, have used the symbolic interactionist perspective in understanding deviant behavior. Particularly important to them has been the concept of the self.[10] Probably most directly influenced by the symbolic interactionist school have been labelling theorists (see, for example, Lemert [1951], Becker [1963], and Schur [1971]). In my opinion, the chief spokesperson for the labelling approach applied to deviance is Edwin Lemert. In his classic work *Social Pathology*, he describes the process whereby a primary deviant (a person who commits a deviant act yet is neither thought of nor thinks of himself as a deviant) becomes a secondary deviant (that is, a person who assumes the role and self-concept of a deviant). Basically, this change occurs because at some point the person is discovered in the commission of a deviant act and is labelled as a deviant.

This process of discovery and labelling is called the "societal reaction." Persons whom the deviant encounters begin to interact with him based on this new role expectation of deviant. That is, they expect the person to act like a deviant. In this interactional nexus the person undergoes subtle and yet profound changes in self-image. He or she takes on the role and self concept (and possibly master status) of the deviant. Many such persons become career deviants and often join with other deviants of like type and form deviant subcultures. (Formation of a subculture is what Lemert refers to as "systematic secondary deviance.")

Labelling theories emphasize the change in the self concept of the individual.[11] Indeed, a fundamental tenet of labelling theory is that the etiology of primary deviance is multifaceted; the causes of the initial behavior are not theoretically interesting to labelling theorists. Rather, the primary point in labelling theory is that the more a person is labelled and continues to be labelled, the more likely that person will act as a deviant and think of him- or herself as a deviant.

Another hallmark of labelling theory, and of others who integrate symbolic interactionist ideas into their own theoretical schema (see, for example, Matza [1969] and Lofland [1969]), is that deviant identities emerge as the result of a process. These theorists argue that the deviant identity emerges from interaction which occurs over time. Whether or not one becomes deviant, therefore, is a complex issue which depends on the reactions of others, the actor's view of self, the situation, and the interactional and social-structural milieu.

Labelling theorists also discuss the processes of isolation and closure. The deviant experiences increasing isolation as he or she is increasingly banned from interaction with nondeviant others. Or at the very least, interaction with nondeviant others is almost exclusively in the role of the newly acquired deviant master status. The deviant may be excluded from occupations, or is generally denied easy access to more conventional roles: he or she undergoes closure. Thus, the person is caught in a deepening spiral wherein he or she is thought of as a deviant and at the same time is not allowed escape into more conventional role playing.[12]

Differential Identification

In an attempt to merge the learning theory concepts of Sutherland's differential association theory of criminality and Mead's perspective, Glaser developed the self-oriented "differential identification theory." Sutherland argued that criminal behavior was learned by persons in the same way that all behavior is learned. A person becomes criminal when there is an excess of definitions favorable to the violation of the law. Seeking to deal with the somewhat specious criticism that differential association theory could not explain criminals who did not interact with criminal groups, Glaser turned to the concept of identification, which he defines as "the choice of another, from whose perspective we view our own behavior" (Glaser, 1956). This definition of identification is then incorporated into the theory of differential identification which posits that a "person pursues criminal behavior to the extent that he identifies himself with real or imaginary persons from whose perspective his criminal behavior seems acceptable" (Glaser, 1956). Such a theory obviously owes a great debt to the concepts of social self and self as being both active and reflexive.

Lindesmith's Theory of Addiction

Alfred Lindesmith, an influential symbolic interactionist, incorporated the concept of self into a major theory of addiction. In *Addiction and Opiates* (1968), Lindesmith differentiated between habituation, which is the organism's physical addiction to narcotics, and addiction. Lindesmith believes that addiction is "reserved for those individuals who have the characteristic craving, whether it is in the form in which it is manifested during regular use or as it exists in the abstaining addict impelling him to resume use" (Lindesmith, 1968: 49). Addiction is also characterized by the high likelihood of relapse even after a person has been physiologically withdrawn from narcotics. A person becomes addicted when he realizes that the distress caused by the withdrawal syndrome is indeed a result of his not continuing to take narcotics. It is only when he associates this distress with the denial of narcotics that he begins to think of himself and act as a narcotic addict. Lindesmith says:

> According to the hypothesis that has been developed here, the sheer physiological or biological effects of drugs are not sufficient to produce addiction although they are indispensable preconditions. The effect which the biological events associated with using drugs has on human behavior is seen as one that is mediated by the manner in which such events are perceived or conceptualized by the person who experiences them. Persons who interpret withdrawal distress as evidence of the onset of an unknown disease act accordingly, and, if they are not enlightened, do not become addicted. Persons who interpret the symptoms of opiate withdrawal as evidence of a need for the drug also act accordingly and, from using the drug after they have understood, become addicted. As the user applies to his own experiences and behavior the attitudes, symbols and sentiments current in his society, he is faced with a problem of adjusting himself to the unpleasant implications of being an addict in a society that defines him as an outcast, pariah, and virtual outlaw. In his efforts to rationalize his own conduct, which he cannot really understand or justify, and to make it more tolerable to himself, he is drawn to others like himself. (Lindesmith, 1968: 95–96)

Thus, Lindesmith points to the crucial importance of the association of withdrawal distress to the formation of the self concept of narcotic addiction and to the formation of the addict subculture.

Summary

This chapter has briefly outlined the major concepts of symbolic interactionist theory and has demonstrated how the approach has been utilized in understanding deviant behavior. Some of the most important concepts that can be distilled from the approach and which will be used in constructing my theory of heroin use, are:

1. The self is both an object and a process. Most notably, the self can act as an object to itself.

2. The self is both enduring and constantly changing.

3. Accordingly, the self has both biographical and situational components.

4. A role is a behavioral expectation. Ego-alter interactions usually occur in what are called "role sets" wherein each actor has a role based on expectations of other's behavior.

5. While behavior which emerges from roles is not completely socially determined, most interactions normally proceed based on roles (expected behavior).

6. All roles and role identities are not equally important to an actor. They are arrayed in a salience hierarchy.

7. To the extent that a person bases his self-identity on a particular role, that person is said to be committed to that role.

8. When a particular role becomes an integral part of a person's identity, almost to the exclusion of all other roles, role merger (or role engulfment) is said to occur. Such a role is often referred to as a "master role."

9. Role conflict exists when the requirements of a role are contradictory or when two or more roles are in conflict with one another.

10. Role strain occurs when a person has a felt difficulty in enacting a role.

11. Reference groups are social groups to which a person looks for role models and for evaluation of his or her behavior. Those members of an actor's reference groups who are most important to him or her are called "significant others."

12. Roles are the basic building blocks of the social structure.

13. Culture is the sum total of language, roles, statuses, norms, and values of the society. Within any complex society subcultures exist, with different values, norms, and roles.

14. Socialization is the process whereby the person learns roles and ultimately develops his or her self-concept. This is a lifelong process.

15. Because socialization is a lifelong process, self-concepts undergo significant changes, even after one becomes an adult.

16. A person comes to think of himself as a deviant when he undergoes societal reaction and thereby becomes a secondary deviant.

17. The acquisition of a deviant identity occurs as a process.

18. The acquisition of a deviant identity occurs through differential identification with deviant others.

19. A person develops a self concept as a narcotic addict partially through recognition that the distress of withdrawal is due to denial of narcotics.

Chapter Three

Towards a Role Theoretic Model of Heroin Use[1]

In this chapter, I first lay out an integrated role theory of heroin use and then demonstrate that the theory is guided and supported by the literature, especially the ethnographically oriented research. This ethnographically informed research—what I have labelled "sociocultural research"—is composed of a growing body of literature which describes what it means to be a heroin addict in urban America. A number of researchers (for example, see Finestone [1964], Sutter [1966], Hughes [1977], Feldman [1968], Waldorf [1973], Agar [1973], Gould, et al. [1974], Rosenbaum [1981], Johnson, et al. [1985], Stephens and Levine [1971], Hendler and Stephens [1977], Stephens and McBride [1976], Preble and Casey [1969], Stephens and Smith [1976], Hanson, et al. [1985], Biernacki [1986], and Weppner [1977]) have argued that chronic heroin use can be viewed as a commitment by the user to a well-defined lifestyle of which drug use is only a part. In addition to these studies by professional social science researchers, there are a number of insightful first person accounts written by members of the street scene. These include works by Brown (1965), Iceberg Slim (1969), Thomas (1967), and Burroughs (1953). Both the professional and first person works forcefully develop one major point: namely, the chronic heroin use lifestyle is so comprehensive and all-encompassing that it constitutes a deviant career for the user (see Dembo et al., 1979; Waldorf, 1973; and Rosenbaum, 1981). While these researchers may differ in some of the particulars, there appears to be a commonality in the various works. The following could be viewed as the central tenets of an emerging sociocultural approach to heroin use:

1. The viewpoint emphasizes the importance of the social context of heroin use: it does not utilize individualistic explanations for heroin use.

2. The viewpoint is nonjudgmental about heroin use and therefore does not rely analytically on concepts generated by the criminal justice system (felon, schedule A drug, etc.) or the medical model (psychopathic deviate, sociopath, schizophrenic, etc.).

3. The sociocultural perspective fits within larger sociological and social-psychological theories (primarily role theory and symbolic interactionism), and the concepts employed in understanding drug use behaviors could apply equally to non-drug use behavior.

4. The approach draws historically from the fields of anthropology and phenomenology and consequently an appreciation of the user's worldview is crucial to the perspective.

5. While not denying the importance of the physiological and psychic effects of heroin, the perspective views neither the negative effects of the drug (withdrawal) nor the seeking of more positive effects (the "high" or the anxiety reducing properties of the substance) as the only—or even primary— explanation for why individuals use heroin.

While the sociocultural approach has produced incredibly rich insight and detail through the use of participant observation or ethnographically informed in-depth interviews, few attempts have been made to develop explicitly a more hypothesis oriented theoretical explanation in which these empirical data could be fitted.[2] As stated earlier, the primary purpose of this book is to create just such a theory of heroin use. This task is to be accomplished by integrating the analytically descriptive sociocultural literature into a more general framework provided by symbolic interaction and role theory.

Towards A Theory

Before I begin to explicate the theory, however, we must devote some attention to the chief dependent variable of the theory—heroin use. As such, the dependent variable is an observable behavior, that is the action of ingesting heroin. I view heroin use as a continuous variable which ranges from no use ever through various levels of experimental and non-regular ("recreational use"), to consistent and chronic use resulting in physical addiction.[3] The term "junkies"[4] refers to individuals who regularly and chronically use heroin and other street drugs.[5] Because of the vagaries of the street life, not all junkies are physically addicted at all times (Goldstein and Duchaine, 1979), although most use heroin in as great a quantity and as frequently as they can. At any one time, the junkie may not use heroin because of a variety of reasons: there is a shortage of heroin on the streets or he or she may be in treatment or in jail. In all likelihood, however, the junkie will eventually return to heroin use. Because of these fluctuations in use, placing a person's behavior on the dependent variable is difficult. One would have to develop an empirically based scheme which takes into account both past behavior (in the recent and more distant past) and current behavior in order to classify any individual on the dependent variable. While this sounds like a difficult—if not impossible—task, it probably can be accomplished by determining the amount of heroin currently being used and the frequency with which it is being consumed. (This, in essence, would be a measure of the extent of use.) If we were studying persons who were in special situations which preclude or limit use of heroin (such as when subjects are incarcerated or hospitalized) we could ask about recent past behavior "while on the streets" to determine extent of use. By looking at these factors, we should be able to score most individuals on the dependent variable.

Having defined the dependent variable, I can now turn to linking it with the independent variables I reviewed in the last chapter. Thus doing, I will generate a number of statements which, taken as a whole, constitute a general role theoretic explanation of heroin use.

Propositions

Proposition 1. There is a subculture of street addicts.

Proposition 2. Within this subculture, a master (or central) role exists, the components of which are organized about the expected use of heroin.

Proposition 3. This master role, called the street addict role, is an ideal type. That is, no one individual exactly meets all of the role requirements so as to be the consummate street addict.[6] However, this master role is highly valued by members of the sub-culture, and the more one's behavior approximates the role, the higher one's status is in the subculture.

Proposition 4. The street addict role provides meaningful social and personal rewards to those who play it.

Proposition 5. There are a number of secondary roles in the subculture which are organized around the master role of street addict. These other roles (such as dealer, tout, steerer, etc.) function to maintain the subculture, especially the status of the master role.

Hypotheses

From the general orientation and the propositions, we can therefore state the major hypothesis of the theory:

Hypothesis 1. *The greater the degree of commitment to the street addict role,*
   the greater will be the extent of heroin use.

Commitment, it will be recalled from Chapter 2, is the degree of investment which a person has both in a certain image of his or her self and in the enactment of certain roles through interaction with others. The more committed a person is to a certain identity or role, the higher the salience of that role.

Remember that *role* and terms dependent upon it, such as *social structure* and *subculture*, as used in this book, are not defined behaviorally. If they were, the theory, of course, would be tautological, since we would be defining both the independent and dependent variables in the same terms. Unfortunately, some of the sociocultural work appears to come close to, falling into this trap, if not actually doing so. Similarly, some of the psychologically oriented work may also come dangerously close to being tautological. In this latter case, the reasoning may go: a person uses heroin because he suffers from some emotional malady, and we know the person suffers from such a malady because he uses heroin. The street addict role is highly salient. The role is prominent (almost to the exclusion of all other roles), has a great level of social support from other junkies, provides both intrinsic and extrinsic social and psychological rewards, and can be enacted successfully in most social situations, including even those not directly related to the subcultural life itself. (For instance, see the discussion by Levine and Stephens [1973] of "games addicts play" in treatment settings.)

Drawing from symbolic interactionism and role theory, a number of other hypotheses can be generated. These include:

Hypothesis 2. *The greater the congruence between the past roles of the actor and street addict role,*

the greater the probability the actor will be socialized into the street addict role.

Hypothesis 3. *The greater the degree of a person's interaction with the street addict culture,*

the greater the degree of commitment to the street addict role.

Hypothesis 4. *The more the person is labelled as a heroin addict,*

the greater the commitment to the street addict role.

Hypothesis 5. *The greater the extent to which the person is cast into the role of street addict,*

the more likely the person is to relapse back into drug use after once leaving the role.

Hypothesis 6. *The greater the role strain felt by the street addict,*

the greater the likelihood the addict will attempt to become abstinent.

Hypothesis 7. *The greater the role conflict felt by the street addict,*

the greater the likelihood that the addict will attempt to become abstinent.

Empirical Test of the Theory

Having laid out the general outlines of the theory, I turn to the sociocultural and other sociological and social-psychological literature[7] to determine if, in fact, there is empirical support for the propositions and hypotheses.[8]

The Street Addict Subculture and Its Rewards
(Prop. 1, Prop. 4)

That there is a street addict subculture cannot be doubted. There are now numerous social-scientific descriptions of the street scene. The descriptions currently available range from article-length analyses (see particularly the now classic article by Preble and Casey [1969]) through descriptions of specific aspects of the life (notably Agar [1973]), to book length treatments of the subject (Rosenbaum, 1981; Gould, et al., 1974; Waldorf, 1973; Johnson, et al., 1985; Hanson, et al., 1985).

All of these works describe a tightly knit world (with relatively well-defined boundaries) that revolves around the expected use of heroin and other street drugs (particularly cocaine, diverted methadone, and other such drugs). The subculture is characterized by a hierarchy of statuses based primarily on conning ability and drug consumption patterns; criminal activities; a great interest in drugs and drug effects, a unique argot which plays both protective and integrative functions; and a set of roles, norms, and values which facilitate and support the manipulative and nonlegal behaviors of addicts. In short, the subculture is a blueprint for what the junkie often sees as an exciting and rewarding life.

Various aspects of the rewards of the life can be documented from the ethnographic studies. Preble and Casey point out:

> Heroin use today by lower class, primarily minority group persons does not provide for them a euphoric escape from the psychological and social problems which derive from ghetto life. On the contrary, it provides a motivation and rationale for the pursuit of a meaningful life, albeit a socially deviant one. The activities these individuals engage in and the relationships they have in the course of their quest for heroin are far more important than the minimal analgesic and euphoric effects of the small amount of heroin available to them. If they can be said to be addicted, it is not so much to heroin as to the entire career of a heroin user. (Preble and Casey, 1969: 21)

Rosenbaum (1981) describes the attraction of the fast-moving and exciting life style to neophyte female heroin users. They were frequently busier—in learning to cop, to hustle, to shoot drugs—than they had ever been in their lives.

Even those only marginally involved in the life, point out that heroin use leads to a series of rewards including: "(1) the thrill of being on the street where by pursuing heroin, they also chose adventure and excitement; (2) a sense of approval from their peers and, if the hustling is successful, a feeling of mastery over particular skills; and (3) a feeling of relief, escape or empowerment which accompanies the effects of heroin, while simultaneously experiencing the distress and complications of heroin use." (Hanson, et al., 1985: 142).

This sociocultural literature describes a world which is vastly different from the relatively secure, middle-class existence most of us know. For the addict, there is great excitement, at times described as "a provocative and captivating environment," but there are also many instances of boredom, discomfort, and danger (Hanson et al., 1985). Addicts are constantly faced with the impending discomfort of withdrawal, reasonably good chances of contracting diseases such as hepatitis, syphilis, and, in some cities, AIDS; danger of physical assault from others in the street scene; and persistent pressures from the criminal justice system.

From the point of view of those not in this subculture, the heroin user's life is a pitiful and harried existence. Many even say participation in the life is a manifestation of mental illness. But most outsiders view the street world through glasses highly colored by traditional cultural values. One of the real strengths of the sociocultural approach—and the field of anthropology from which it is drawn—is that it points out our own cultural biases. It forcefully makes the point that simply because nonparticipants do not find meaning in the life does not mean that it in fact has no meaning. The rewards and costs of any lifestyle must be viewed through the eyes of those who live it. Socioculturally oriented observers make the points that the addict lifestyle is meaningful and rewarding to street addicts and that it can most wholly be understood in the specific social context in which it flourishes.

As Dembo, et al. comment in their study of adolescent drug users (most of whom are primarily, but not exclusively, marihuana users) who live in a high drug use area:

> The results show convincingly that the drug use of the youths we studied is incorporated into the manner in which they relate to their environment. Rather than reflecting a sense of aberration from their social settings, the students' drug taking reflects motivated, valued behavior that is associated with a number of reinforcing attitudes, cultural orientations, out of school activities, friends' drug behavior—as well as personal experience with the consequences [of] their use of substances....
>
> Basic to the thrust of our argument is the recognition that we must cease regarding drug use as reflecting primarily personality and interpersonal problems...However, drug taking must be viewed as an environmentally related phenomenon that serves to define a personal and social self in a particular social and cultural setting. (Dembo et al., 1978: 246-247)

This same insight has been gained by researchers dealing with other forms of deviant behavior. In a recent review of some classic research on nondelinquent youth ("good boys") in a high delinquency area, Stryker and Craft commented: "Further, it appeared that the study had failed to appreciate the possibility that, to an important degree, it is the lower-class black "good boy" who is deviant (in terms of the norms of the local society that is the content of his actions)" (Stryker and Craft, 1982: 169).

While the above points have almost become sociological and anthropological cliches, it seems that both the public and many professionals in the drug field continue to subscribe to the view that heroin use is indicative of underlying psychopathology. Obviously, the present theory rejects the psychopathological explanation of heroin use, and I will deal more extensively with this point in a later chapter.

The Components of the Street Addict Role
(Prop. 2, 3, and 5)

As I have said, the principal role in the "life" is that of the street addict. But does such a role exist? In 1971, Stephen Levine, a psychiatrist colleague, and I reviewed the available literature in an attempt to identify the characteristics of the street addict role. While our description is now almost two decades old—and, as noted earlier, there may have been some changes in the street scene—my reading of the most recent literature would indicate that this description of the role is still, by and large, valid. We saw the street addict role then as consisting of three major components: a "cool cat" syndrome, a positive view of conning behavior and an anti-societal viewpoint.[9] Briefly, we saw the "cool cat" as one who displays little social concern or guilt for his actions, values the outward display of material goods and other signs of success, admires an easy ability to communicate in street language, values excitement[10], does not believe in long-range planning[11], condemns snitching, and generally eschews the use of violence.[12] Also highly evaluated in the addict subculture is the ability to "con," that is, to skillfully trick others into providing money, drugs, sex, or other things the addict desires. High status is conferred on those who are most adept at conning. Finally, the street addict is expected to have an anti-societal viewpoint—that is, to feel persecuted in a world that is peopled by dishonest and insincere persons. And, of course, the street addict values highly the use of heroin and other street drugs.[13]

Can we behaviorally differentiate street addicts from other heroin users? One such attempt (Stephens and Slatin, 1974) operationalized the street addict role (using a series of behaviors as the measurement of the role).[14] Street addicts were compared with other narcotic users and addicts who were less socialized and less committed to street addict role. This study, conducted among patients at the Federal narcotics hospital in Lexington, Kentucky, defined the street addict role as consisting of the following behaviors: (1) used more than one type of narcotic; (2) had been arrested at least once; (3) had engaged in at least one felony; (4) had used illegal drug sources (such as pusher rather than friend); (5) had most frequently used the intravenous route (a demonstrable measure of significant involvement in narcotics use); (6) had "kicked" at least once other than the present detoxification at Lexington; (7) preferred (or most frequently used) heroin or cocaine; and (8) had sold drugs at least once. Of the 1,096 narcotics users in the sample, 32 percent (350) could be classified as street addicts. 64 percent (224) of these street addicts were from minority groups (primarily Blacks, since Hispanics were underrepresented in Lexington's population). Meaningful differences were found between street addicts and other addicts on a whole host of other variables. Street addicts were more likely than other addicts to have:

1. used marihuana.

2. first used marihuana at a younger age.

3. been addicted to narcotics at a younger age.

4. used intravenously the first time they used narcotics.

5. obtained narcotics illegally when they were first addicted.

6. used the intravenous route regularly at an earlier age.

7. used a greater number of drugs in their last month on the street prior to hospitalization at Lexington.

8. had a larger daily cost for drugs in their last month on the street.

9. been arrested a greater number of times.

We concluded:

> First, the street addict role seems to be synonymous with the concept of the career deviant. The street addict, of all narcotic addicts, is most committed to and involved in the drug subculture. His adherence to the unique combination of behaviors which constitute this role suggests that he is a street addict to the exclusion of all other roles. In short, his behavior is almost completely determined by this one role.
>
> Second, this commitment of the street addict has important typological implications. The street addict represents one end of a continuum of narcotic abusers. With the establishment of the end point of this typological continuum, it may be possible to develop a classification scheme, using various combinations of these eight variables, which would include the other two-thirds of the patients in this sample. (Stephens and Slatin, 1974: 386–387.)

What this study and the previously cited sociocultural literature demonstrate is that the street addict role and the role behaviors associated with it have empirical referents.

Besides the master role of the street addict, there are a number of subroles in the subculture. Sutter (1966) describes a whole host of drug-distribution and criminally related roles in the world of the "righteous dope fiend". Preble and Casey (1969) also describe the various levels of drug distribution roles as well as a number of other specialists such as lieutenants, testers, drop men, salesmen, steerers, taste faces, and accommodators. These and other descriptions point out the myriad subroles which are organized either to facilitate drug distribution or to aid in the illegal acquisition of money. Also to be found in the subculture are others who, while not necessarily users, are nevertheless important to supporting the lifestyle. These would include pimps, prostitutes, fences, professional thieves, doctors who knowingly sell drugs to addicts, and a whole host of other players on the street scene.

There are a large number of nondeviant others who also are part of the scene. Among these are persons who would not really consider themselves members of the subculture, yet have important effects upon the subculture and help shape it in many significant ways. These include members of the criminal justice system (police, courts, and probation officers) and drug treatment personnel. (For an account of their views, see Gould, et al. [1974].)

Street Addict Values (Propositions 2 and 3)

One way to document the existence of both the subculture and the role is to determine the structure of the values in the subculture and its correspondence to the role requirements. In a factor anaytic study of 516 addicts in treatment (Stephens, Levine, and Ross, 1976), six factors were extracted from a list of forty-seven values statements to which the addicts responded. The six factors constitute the main tenets of the value system of subculture. They are:

Factor 1—*Antisociety viewpoint*—This dimension of the value system reflects the notion that people are basically dishonest and egocentric. The factor also indicates the cynicism of the addict about non-addict others.

Factor 2—*Rejection of middle class values* indicates the denigration of the alleged "square life" ideals of hard work, security and honesty. In fact, this factor is so well defined that one is tempted to assert that the addict subculture is almost a contraculture.

Factor 3—*Excitement-hedonism* represents some of the elements of the "cool cat" pattern. Again, the factor appears to measure the "square-addict" dichotomy with the addict lifestyle being a much more exciting and intense response to life. The factor structure strongly suggests that addicts do endorse the fast life and pursuit of immediate gratification with little thought given to the future.

Factor 4—*Importance of outward appearances* indicates that the addict subscribes to the conspicuous consumption mode of life. Money, clothes, and cars are to be used for image management as much for any intrinsic worth they may have.

Factor 5—*Valence of street addict subcultures* appears to indicate the importance of addict friends and involvement in the addict subculture. Rather than noting possible dangers inherent in membership in the addict subculture, the factor seems to measure the allegiance which even a "clean" addict is supposed to have to his addict friends.

Factor 6—"Cool cat" emphasizes the addict's emotional aloofness. It makes the point that weakness is defined as being emotionally liable to other persons. In other words, one should never "open up" to others. (Stephens, Levine, and Ross, 1976: 278)

From the foregoing analysis, it is clear that there is a rather large amount of overlap between the values expressed by these addicts and the role expectations of the street addict.[15]

Commitment to the Role (**Hypothesis 1**)

The greater the degree of commitment to the street addict role, the greater will be the extent of heroin use.

Having demonstrated empirical support for the theory's propositions, we come now to an empirical test of the major hypothesis. Several authors have shown that as commitment to the life (and the street addict role) increases, so does the extent of heroin use.[16]

Commitment is the extent to which one is invested in a particular self-image. It can be measured either directly or it can be inferred from behavior. An underlying theme of many psychological and social-psychological theories of drug use is that the person becomes committed to a drug user self-image.[17] The ethnographic literature identifies the point at which a salient social identity is part and parcel of what it means to be an addict. As Waldorf says:

What then are the dope fiends? They are for the most part urban addicts who are overwhelmed by their addiction and must hustle on a sustained and continual basis to support their drug needs. The combination of uncontrolled drug use and regular hustling—in juxtaposition with the larger culture's mores, laws and values about drug use—causes the development of a social identity *distinct from addiction,* [italics mine] which in a larger social context is seen as the addict subculture. Those addicts who somehow do not identify with the subculture are not, according to addicts, dope fiends; those who do, are dope fiends. (Waldorf, 1973: 17)

At least one study has empirically demonstrated that the self-concept of addicts seems very salient to many addicts, thus indicating commitment to the role. McAuliffe (1975) reports in a study of fifty-nine male narcotics addicts that "When asked to complete the sentence: 'I am_____,' the *only response* [italics mine] given by more than one respondent was 'I am a drug addict.' This response was given by twenty-four subjects. Clearly, they have adopted the addict self-concept as a result of their own or someone else's labeling" (McAuliffe, 1975: 207). In other words, they have a fair degree of investment in a certain image of themselves—they are committed to being street addicts.

Commitment can also be inferred from the behaviors of addicts. Rosenbaum (1981) sees the female addict as becoming socially inundated (what I called "role engulfment" in Chapter 2) by her activities as an addict. By this she means that, because of the lifestyle, the addict builds "safe social networks." She chiefly associates with people who are "all right"—that is, other addicts. This isolation from non-using others usually means that eventually the "entire world begins to look strung out" (Rosenbaum, 1981: 53). Rosenbaum discusses time inundation, as well. "The heroin life is so chaotic that heroin-related activities preoccupy the addict. She is too busy hustling, scoring, and administering heroin to have time to do what many women have called normal things" (Rosenbaum, 1981: 57).

The Congruence of the Street Addict Role With Other Deviant Roles (Hypothesis 2)

Hypothesis 2. *The greater the congruence between the past roles of the actor and the street addict role,*
the greater the probability the actor will be socialized into the street addict role.

The process of becoming a street addict usually begins in the mid-teens to the early twenties. In order to comprehend the process, we must utilize the concept of "adult socialization." Adult socialization is basically a process of synthesizing elements learned earlier into new forms and combinations of skills. In essence, adult socialization is the "trying on" of new roles and, at times, new self-concepts. When one of these new role identities does not fit, it is "sloughed off" (McCall and Simmons, 1978: 219). While this helps to explain why a person *does not* select certain roles and role identities, its obverse may also help us to understand why a person *chooses* certain role identities. It seems to me that a person is more likely to adopt new role identities (or roles) when these are compatible with existing roles and self-concepts.

That this is true of addicts is illustrated by Rosenbaum's (1981) work on female heroin addicts. She discusses the three worlds from which most of her female addict subjects came prior to their entry into the world of heroin. The first is the "hippie trip" where drug use and unconventional behavior are highly valued. Second, there is the "outlaw world" characterized by an emphasis on toughness, violence, partying, drug use, and other gang oriented activities. Finally, there is the "fast life"—often appealing to women with what they perceive to be a glamorous life of prostitution —consisting of high living, conspicuous consumption, and sustained excitement. These three life-styles share, in varying degrees, commonality with the street addict subculture. They fit with self-images and roles already developed, and the psychic and behavioral cost of integrating them into the existing repertoire of roles is minimal.

Similarly, a study contrasting heroin addicts with their non-addicted brothers found that the addicted siblings were temperamentally and behaviorally more predisposed to becoming addicts (Maddux and Desmond, 1984). That is, addicted siblings, prior to their drug dependence, had been more rebellious and bad-tempered, and had engaged in many more nonconventional activities as youngsters than did their nonaddicted brothers. They also had associated more with deviant peers. In short, the "role jump" from non-drug using deviant to heroin user appears to have been "shorter" for the siblings who became addicted than for those who did not. In other words, previous roles for the addicted sibling were more compatible for the heroin user than for his nonaddicted brother.

Factors Affecting Commitment to the Street Addict Role

Hypothesis 3. *The greater the degree of a person's interaction with the street addict culture,*
  the greater the degree of commitment to the street addict role.
Hypothesis 4. *The more the person is labelled as a heroin addict,*
  the greater the degree of commitment to the street addict role.
These two hypotheses partially specify the ways in which a person becomes committed to the street addict role. They basically illustrate two sides of the same coin. For as we shall see, increasing commitment to the street addict role is a product of increasing identification and interaction with significant others who themselves are addicts and a decline in interaction and identification with nonaddict significant others.

As I pointed out in the previous chapter, learning of values, norms, and behaviors occurs in a group context. This is nowhere more true than in the case of heroin users who begin to differentially associate with street addict norms, values, and behaviors. Many neophyte users increasingly identify with addicts while they simultaneously come to devalue the norms and values of nonaddict significant others. They also come to take on new self-concepts and the role behaviors congruent with these new self-concepts. Further, as Hypothesis 4 predicts, nonaddict significant others come to define the users as street addicts and consequently change their behavior towards the users. In turn, rejection by nonaddict significant others leads to further identification with addicts. Lemert (1951) calls this the "process of isolation and closure." In essence, the user is "pulled" into commitment to the street addict role by new addict significant others while at the same time is "pushed" by the changed and largely negative reaction of non-addict significant others.

The literature clearly documents these processes. Rosenbaum, for instance, describes the process thusly:

> The risks in the heroin routine—from hustling to fixing—force addicts to insulate their world, and because of this insulation, they lose touch with individuals and social groups that are not part of the heroin world. Their own personal use of heroin and the narrow views of other addicts begin to dominate their thinking and perspective. Although many women complained that due to the risk involved in becoming close to addicts, they lacked solid friendships, their associations were composed almost wholly of other addicts. Fellow addicts may be threatening and untrustworthy, but it is worse to try to interact with squares who have no trust, understanding, or respect for addicts. Nonaddicts tend to lump them into a singular, stereotypical category of rip-offs and low-lifes. (Rosenbaum, 1981: 60)

McAuliffe also documents the role that nonaddict significant others play in funneling addicts into commitment to the street addict way of life. He writes:

> When informal social relations were considered, we found that wives always knew about their husbands' addiction, and the addicts' mothers usually knew. Addiction was often a cause of divorce or separation, and those wives who did not break off kept pressure on their husbands to stop. The addicts said that their desire to live a normal married life was a major reason for wanting to get off drugs. Many friends were lost as a result of the respondent's involve-ment with drugs and even those nonaddicts who were will-

ing to remain friendly merely tolerated the addicts' deviance. Enthusiastic support was never described. While relatives of the addicts did not approve of addiction, they directed their pressure at the addicts' parents. The only family members who were known to reject the addicts outright were their fathers, and this seemed to be a function of the generally poor relationships between sons and fathers in these families. Neighbors, who often knew that the respondents were addicted, avoided them whenever possible. (McAuliffe, 1975: 223)

Two other studies (Stephens and McBride, 1976; Hendler and Stephens, 1977) demonstrated the process of increasing salience of the street addict role and the important role of significant others in shaping this commitment. During the typical one year period between first use and addiction—known on the street as the "honeymoon"—there is an increasing amount of involvement with user friends and a decrease in interaction with significant others. In detailed interviews with fifty institutionalized black male addicts, Stephens and McBride (1976) assessed these subjects' behavioral patterns at three points in time: before first narcotics use, immediately after first use, and after addiction to narcotics. The study found that:

1. the percentage of time spent with addicts increases.

2. the subjects increasingly avoid interaction with nonaddict significant others (family and non-addict friends.)

3. nonaddict significant others increasingly avoid the subjects.

4. involvement in criminal activities increases.

5. involvement in other nondeviant activities (attendance in school or legal employment) decreases.

Clearly what we see is the process of role merger or role engulfment. Users become increasingly involved in a world where the nature and number of their role sets—already limited as the result of economic and often racial discrimination—are even more limited. Former significant others who are not involved in the drug world both reject this lifestyle and in turn are rejected by the addict. Slowly, the most important significant other group becomes that of other addicts. Addicts come more and more to organize both their behavior and their self-concepts about the role of street addict. In essence, the street addict role assumes a master status for these individuals, for they come both to judge themselves and be judged by others based on this highly salient role.

The Phenomenon of Relapse (Hypothesis 5)

Hypothesis 5. *The greater the extent to which the person is cast into the role of street addict, the more likely the person is to relapse back into drug use after once leaving the role.*

Role theory, and especially labelling theory, can help us to understand one of the most common phenomena observed among addicts: relapse.[18] A number of researchers have pointed to the importance of others' influence in the occurrence of relapse. [19] A study contrasting those who relapsed with abstainers found that if a person's self-identity as an abstainer is not supported by others, the likelihood of relapse increases.

In the period following physical withdrawal from heroin, the addict attempts to enact a new social reality which coincides with this desired self-image as an abstainer, and he seeks ratification of his new identity from others in the situations he faces. But the abstainer's social expectations during a period when he is off drugs are frequently not gratified. Here again, socially disjunctive experiences bring about a questioning of the value of an abstainer identity and promote reflections in which addict and non-addict identities and relationships are compared. The abstainer's realignment of his values with those of the world of addiction results in the redefinition of self as an addict and has as a consequence the actions necessary to relapse. But it should be noted that the seeds of a new attempt at abstinence are sown, once addiction has been re-established, in the self-recriminations engaged in upon remembrance of a successful period of abstinence (Ray, 1964: 175–177).

Others have reported similar findings. Waldorf (1976) reports that persons who were treated as addicts during abstention were more likely to relapse than were those who were not so treated. He cautions, however, that the cause and effect relationships were not clear.

In a detailed test of the relationship between labelling and relapse, Stephens (1971) found that 25 percent of the variance in relapse could be accounted for by three variables—continued labelling as an addict by family, nonaddict friends, and addict friends. Labelling was measured by whether significant others said and acted as though they suspected the research subjects had already used narcotics when, in fact, they had not. Basically, if these three groups of significant others interacted with the abstinent person as an addict before he had reused drugs, he was much more likely to relapse than if he was not so treated.

The Dynamics of Abstinence

Hypothesis 6. *The greater the role strain felt by the street addict, the greater the likelihood that an attempt is made to become abstinent.*

A very important event in an addict's life occurs when the person voluntarily gives up—on his or her own—the use of heroin. (Enforced abstinence, as when persons are incarcerated, often lasts only as long as the street addict lacks access to heroin.) Why do addicts voluntarily give up heroin? I would argue that Hypotheses 6 and 7 propose a reason for this behavior change. Hypothesis 6 posits that when addicts experience role strain (vis a vis their street addict role), they are more likely to attempt abstinence. Role strain, as defined in the previous chapter, is a felt difficulty in enacting the requirements of a role.

Addicts often experience problems in enacting the role when their habits become unmanageably large. The term "greasy dope fiend" refers to those who cannot present the proper image on the street because all of their energies and resources have been spent simply in "feeding their habit." This increase in illegal or deviant behaviors is reflected in the finding (Ellis and Stephens, 1976) that arrest rates rise dramatically for addicts in the one year period before their admission into treatment. I interpret these data as indicating that more and more energy goes into criminal activity as one's habit grows. The chance of arrest heightened due to increased criminal activity. When one no longer can adequately play the role, one is more likely to seek at least a brief respite offered by detoxification and treatment.

One detailed and fascinating study of 101 persons who achieved abstinence without treatment, reported that most of the subjects made an explicit and rational decision to stop using opiates (Biernacki, 1986). They resurrected old pre-addiction identities or, when this was not possible, they created new nonaddict roles and self-concepts. Some undertook this path to abstinence either because their increasing use was inconsistent with lingering nonaddict identities or because they feared the ultimate physical and social consequences of their addiction. (These individuals are really more appropriate examples of those who experience role conflict, and they will be discussed in the next chapter.) Others sought abstinence because they had "burned out" on the lifestyle. They were "tired of 'the life', the 'changes,' of other junkies and of going to jail" (Biernacki, 1986: 53). In my view, this means the addict feels role strain—a felt inability to continue to enact the requirements of the role and lifestyle.

Hypothesis 7. *The greater the role conflict felt by the street addict, the greater the likelihood that an attempt is made to become abstinent.*

Role conflict, as described in Chapter 2, usually occurs when the behaviors demanded by one role are contradictory or inconsistent with the demands of another role. The attempt to become abstinent may be the result of such a conflict with their current role. The clearest example of such role conflict is Rosenbaum's (1981) characterization of the agonizing choices that an addicted mother must make between the all-consuming role demands of a junkie versus a mother. Often the guilt experienced by these women builds to the breaking point and they finally seek out treatment.

Another type of role conflict occurs when persons' self-images conflict with those of their roles. Some persons leave the drug life because either they have hit "rock bottom" or they undergo an "existential crisis" (Biernacki, 1986). In the former case, individuals believe they have reached the nadir of their lives and decide that the addict lifestyle is intolerable. In the latter case, the existential crisis is a more profound emotional and psychological state, except that it too involves the decision to abandon the street addict self-concept. In this case, one comes to believe that one's true self is not compatible with the addict self-concept.

In the final analysis, then, the seeking of abstinence is found to fit with the symbolic interactionist/role theory framework proposed here. It involves the attempted abandonment of the addict self concept either because the role has become too demanding or it is in conflict with other previous roles or newly emergent ones. "Natural recovery refers to the process through which a new calculus or arrangement of identities and perspectives emerges and becomes relatively stabilized. This process entails a different articulation of identities in which the identity as an addict becomes deemphasized (symbolically and socially) relative to other identities existing or emerging as part of the person's overall life arrangement" (Biernacki, 1986: 25).

We have now completed a review of the theory's propositions and hypotheses. I hope I have convinced you that the theory is supported by the empirical literature. As noted early on in this chapter, even more empirical support will be found in the next chapter when we review the process of becoming a street addict.

Nonaddicted Heroin Users

Much of the work cited here has focused on those who would be considered heavily addicted narcotic users. As such, I have not alluded much to the other types of narcotic users who represent different levels of use. Partly, this lack of attention to other users is due to the literature. The vast bulk of the studies are concerned primarily with addicts and addiction. As I have shown, however, even among addicted persons there are degrees of addiction (size of habit, length of heroin use, etc.).

There is a smaller body of literature which deals with persons who are not addicted. Every person familiar with the heroin subculture is aware of the "chipper" or "chippie" who is usually a novice heroin user, possibly on the way to becoming a full-fledged addict. Sometimes chippers want to become addicts but cannot do so because of the poor quality of the narcotics (Delgaty, 1976). Or they may not have whatever it takes to become a junkie. Gay and his associates (1973), for instance, have documented the existence of "pseudo-junkies"—persons who want to be part of the heroin scene yet don't quite make it. Typically, they use heroin sporadically, and they exaggerate the extent of their use in order to be considered part of the subculture.

McKay (1980) studied four types of heroin users in Cheyenne, Wyoming. These were addicts, former addicts, concerned nonaddicts (so called because they are concerned about becoming physically addicted to heroin), and unconcerned nonaddicts (who appear not to be troubled about the prospect of physical addiction). McKay found that the addicts and concerned nonaddicts anchored opposite ends of a continuum. The addicts were most deviant in terms of their lifestyle. They were less educated, more likely to be unemployed, heavily involved in criminal activities to support their habits, and less involved in other conventional activities. The concerned nonaddicts, on the other hand, were very bonded to conventional activities. They were more likely to be high school graduates, avoided engaging in illegal activities, and expressed concern about the consequences of heroin use on their job and families. They did not plan to use heroin extensively.

The two other groups fell between these two extremes. Trends were difficult to discern for the former addicts, possibly because some were probably moving toward increased drug use while others were pointed toward diminished use. The unconcerned nonaddict, while similar to the concerned nonaddict in terms of education, employment, and lack of prior heroin treatment or overdose episodes, was more deviant than the concerned nonaddict. He or she interacted more with other addicts, expressed minimal concern about the consequences of heroin use and engaged in more illegal activities.

To my way of thinking, what we see here are various degrees of both commitment to the addict lifestyle (*not extent of heroin use*) and estrangement from conventional society. What clearly emerges is that commitment to the addict lifestyle predicts extent of heroin use among these heterogeneous narcotic users. These data provide further support for the major hypothesis of the theory.

In 1985 Bill Hanson and his colleagues George Beschner, James W. Walters, and Elliot Bovelle wrote *Life With Heroin* (1985), which is a rich, ethnographically informed interview study of 124 black inner-city heroin users who had never been in treatment. In order to be included in the study, these men had to have injected heroin at least once a day for at least eight days in the two weeks prior to their interview. Most used the drug no more than once a day (Hanson et al.: 177). Eighty-five percent of these men spent no more than thirty dollars a day for heroin use. About one-fourth reported that their main source of income was legitimate work. The rest earned their way chiefly through theft, drug sales, and a variety of other hustles, most of which consisted of petty crime. These men thus could be considered "marginal," living wholly neither in the addict subculture nor in the straight world (see Hanson, et al., 1985: 149).

Part of the theme of *Life With Heroin* is that the heroin street scene has changed, and that these "part-time" junkies are more representative of the street scene. However, as I have noted elsewhere, Hansen et al. do not develop this theme to its fullest (see Stephens, 1986). I believe it is striking how the study's findings fit into the general theory proposed here. Rather than viewing the "part-time" junkies as the new "representatives" of the street scene, perhaps it might be more fruitful to see them simply as less committed to the street addict scene. Indeed, Hanson and his associates (1985) seem to be saying this in the following passage:

> They see themselves as neither down-and-out nodding, dehumanized junkies nor as the glamorous elite "cool cats" of the drug world. A basic aspect of their self-perception is their refusal to consider themselves as true

denizens of the drug world, but rather as individuals who move confidently in and between both the drug and straight worlds. Indeed, much of their reported behavior lends support to their rejection of the addict stereotype as applied to themselves. (Hanson et al., 1985: 178)

It is not surprising, then, that because they are not fully committed to the street addict role, their heroin use is "controlled, most often consisting of only one shot a day" (Hanson et al., 1985: 177).

Even further removed from the street scene are the heroin users studied by Zinberg and his associates in a number of research projects (Zinberg, et al., 1977; Zinberg, et al., 1975; Zinberg, 1979; Zinberg, 1984). In studying controlled users[20], Zinberg found that the users developed a set of sanctions and rituals which help to control use. These sanctions and rituals are both attitudinal and behavioral and are especially focused on the social setting in which narcotics are used. The functions of these sanctions and rituals are:

1. Sanctions define moderate use and condemn compulsive use. (Most of the subjects follow sanctions that limit use to frequencies well below those required for addiction. Many have special sanctions, such as "Don't use every day" or "Never use on more than two consecutive days.")
2. Sanctions limit use to physical and social settings that are conducive to a positive or "safe" drug experience. (Some subjects refuse to use in the company of addicts from whom they have bought the drug, and most avoid driving a car when high.)
3. Sanctions and rituals identify potentially untoward drug effects and prescribe precautions to be taken before and during use. (Some subjects minimize the risk of an overdose by using only a portion of their drug and waiting to gauge its effect before taking more. Others avoid mixing certain drugs, boil their works before injection, or refuse to share works.)

4. Sanctions and rituals operate to compartmentalize drug use and support the users' everyday obligations and relationships. (Some subjects avoid using opiates on Sunday night so that they will not be too tired to go to work on Monday morning. Some carefully budget the amount of money they spend on drugs.) (Zinberg, 1979: 309)

In terms of my theory, these sanctions and rituals effectively serve to limit the level of commitment to the street addict role. In fact, for Zinberg's occasional user, the lifestyle of addicts is significantly devalued, and these rituals and sanctions are adhered to in order to distance themselves from "junkie type" viewpoints and behavior. Further, occasional users maintain many more contacts with both nonusers and controlled users than do the more compulsive users (Zinberg, 1984).

Yet another study of both addicted persons and occasional narcotic users is Robins's (1973) influential research on returning Vietnam veterans. Despite relatively significant experience with narcotics and other drugs (Robins estimates that at least 34 percent of the soldiers in Vietnam had used heroin and 38 percent had used opium while there), use of narcotics upon return to the United States declined markedly. The single best predictors of heavy use of narcotics after discharge were: injection of narcotics before Vietnam; parent(s) who were alcoholic, had been arrested or who were drug users; and heavy drug use by the subject before entering the service. All of these factors could be seen as either direct measures of potential commitment to the street addict lifestyle (particularly use of the intravenous route) or at least as indicators of a milieu favorable to the development of an allegiance to the street addict way of life.

In summary, this literature on persons who do not use narcotics to the extent of a fully committed street addict seems to indicate—without too much "stretching" of the data—that the hypotheses developed herein are supported. Obviously, much more research on persons who score lower on the heroin use dependent variable needs to be conducted.

Summary

In this chapter I have developed, both inductively and deductively, a theory of heroin use. Clearly, the central construct of the theory is the street addict role. While the theory clearly runs the danger of falsely reifying this concept, I think that the data presented indicate the role (in the broad, "ideal type" form conceptualized here) has empirical referents and constitutes a model around which street addicts pattern their behavior. It seems clearly to predict levels of heroin use.

In the next chapter, we will explore how one comes to be a street addict. Further empirical support will be garnered in support of the theory as we study this process of becoming and being a street addict.

Chapter Four

Becoming and Being a Street Addict

A number of drug researchers (Waldorf [1973], Winick [1974], and Robins [1979], among others) have applied the concept of career deviance (Becker, 1963) to narcotics addicts. As we have seen, the general idea is that the junkie becomes committed to this identity and organizes his or her behavior about this master status. As with most careers, there are stages through which the person passes. These stages for the full-fledged street addict include:

1. Recruitment into initial heroin use—The antecedent factors involved in deciding to first use heroin.

2. First use—The reasons for and social circumstances of first use.

3. The Honeymoon—Increasing involvement with heroin beyond the experimental stage.

4. First addiction—The time at which physical addiction is realized for the first time.

5. Life as a junkie—The demanding lifestyle of the addict including both hustling and copping.

6. Leaving the life—The time when most decide the lifestyle is too demanding and decide to abandon the role.

In this chapter I shall review these career stages in great detail, citing the research studies which have been conducted. I shall also point out how these studies lend further support to the general theoretical model being proposed here.

Circumstances of First Use

Differences Between Users and Nonusers

All journeys commence with a first step. The addict odyssey begins when the person first uses heroin. Who decides to take that first step? Some research has focused on this question by contrasting the different career pathways of users and nonusers from similar backgrounds.[1] One such study contrasted sixty-five Washington, D.C., black heroin-using youth with a like number of nonusers matched on race, age, sex, and education (Craig and Brown, 1975). Family background, current family relationships, community adjustment, and drug use were studied. It was found that there was great similarity of early childhood experiences (community activities, church attendance, school experiences, etc.), except that drug users were significantly more likely to have been raised in single parent families. Family instability was high in both groups, but it was more intense for drug users at an earlier age. Users' families were significantly more likely to be involved with drugs than those of nonusers (40 percent vs. 8 percent). Many of the other differences between the two groups (such as drug users having fewer friends and higher school dropout rates) were more likely the result rather than the cause of drug use.

Another study examined a sample of 235 young black men, ages thirty to thirty-five whose names were selected from St. Louis, Missouri, public elementary school records which predated the study by twenty-six to thirty years (Robins and Murphy, 1967). These men were then traced to determine whether they currently used drugs. Thirteen percent reported having tried heroin and 10 percent became addicted to it. Interestingly, every man who used heroin more than six times said he became addicted to it. In attempting to isolate those factors which accounted for future drug use, it was found that childhood situations (occupational status of the guardian, adjustment to school, and presence or absence of the father) were not predictive by themselves of future drug use. Some educational variables, however, were related to future drug use. Twice as many high school dropouts as graduates used drugs. Boys

who had never attended high school used drugs about as infrequently as did the graduates. More than one-third of the high
school dropouts who used marihuana also used heroin. Those with
police or juvenile court records before age seventeen were significantly more likely to be drug users. In constructing profiles of
future drug users, "Being a drop-out seems to be a major determi-
nant of experimentation with drugs, while delinquency and having
no father in the home seem to be major determinants of going on
to heroin addiction once drugs are tried" (Robins and Murphy
1967: 1593). "The combination of the absent father, delinquency and
dropping out of high school characterized the group of boys most
vulnerable to heroin addiction" (Robins and Murphy, 1967: 1596).

Glaser, et al. (1971) contrasted forty pairs of addict and nonaddict siblings of the same sex who were eighteen years of age or
older. They concluded typical addicts were different from their
nonaddict siblings in that they were more involved at a younger
age in delinquency and marihuana use. Addicts also were arrested
and incarcerated more often, received less schooling, and had
poorer employment records. Fewer differences were discovered in
the home situation, but the addict was more likely to have resided
in a slum at an earlier age and to have stayed at home less than the
nonaddicted sibling. "What was most clearly indicated is the difference in early reference group orientation in these sibling pairs.
The addicts were highly involved in the illegitimate opportunity
structure of the street at an early age, with arrest and incarceration
consequences that would be long-run barriers to mobility in legitimate careers. Contrastingly, the nonaddicts early eschewed the
illegitimate world and sought conventional employment" (Glaser,
1971: 519).

As reported in the earlier chapter, women heroin addicts were
more likely to be recruited from three deviant worlds:

1. the "hippie trip" where drug use and unconventional
behavior are highly valued. (This route was especially
characteristic of middle class women.)

2. the "outlaw world" which was characterized by an emphasis on toughness, violence, partying, drug use, and other
group oriented activities.

3. the "fast life" of the prostitute, which consisted of high living, conspicuous consumption, and sustained excitement. (Rosenbaum, 1981)

Yet another study contrasted three groups of black males: those who had been addicted to heroin, those who experimented with it, and those who had never used it (Crawford, Washington, and Senay, 1980). Addicts were more likely than the other two groups to have come from broken homes, reported problems with their parent(s), associated with friends who were involved in serious drug use and other illegal activities, dropped out of school, and possessed either no goals or no socially accepted goals in life. Many of the above differences, while in the predicted direction, were not statistically significant. This lack of significant difference may be due to the possibility that many of the social disharmony indicators (broken homes, dropping out of school, deviant behavior, etc.) may be so pervasive as to be the norm in the ghetto.

Another study conducted in Texas contrasted the addict with their nonaddicted siblings (Maddux and Desmond, 1984). It found that when they were compared to their nonaddicted siblings, addicts were more rebellious, resentful, hot-tempered and aggressive. They were much more likely to have associated with drug users and were less involved in conventional activities. In short, their pre-addiction circumstances seem to have created their future drug use.

Similarly, a study of two hundred currently addicted street prostitutes found their subjects had drifted gradually into deviance (Silbert, Pines, and Lynch, 1982). While 27 percent of them reported that in grammar school they had friends who were deviant, that figure had risen to 78 by the time the subjects reached high school. The overall picture is one of lonely, isolated young girls who turn to deviant friends where they do not experience rejection.

These studies, taken as a whole, indicate that many heroin users are drawn from the ranks of those who already are seen as deviant. They experimented with other drugs prior to their heroin use and their role models were drug users. They were limited in the number and variety of roles they could play. Because of their temperament, their lack of education and their involvement in delinquency, they began to develop behaviors and self-concepts which already were compatible with the requirements of the street addict role. Thus many of those who choose to use heroin already possess prior roles and self-concepts which are congruent with the street addict role. Such findings constitute additional support for Hypothesis 2 of this theory.

Reasons for First Use

Various researchers attempted to understand—from the addicts' perspective—why they first used narcotics. One found that curiosity and the influence of significant others (friends, relatives, etc.) were the chief reasons given for first use of heroin while other less frequent responses were "relief of personal disturbance" and "seeking a high" (Brown, et al., 1971). Another also reported that "curiosity to experiment" and "to go along with others" were the chief reasons advanced for first heroin use (Stephens and McBride, 1976). Similarly, "social pressure" or "curiosity" were the major reasons provided for their first use by addicts studied by Hendler and Stephens (1977) and Hanson, et al. (1985).

Of these two (curiosity vs. social pressure), researchers identified the influence of significant others as the chief factor in initial use. One study (Gibbons, et al., 1981) reported that almost three-fourths of novices had been initiated to heroin use by close friends. Some persons are susceptible to such social pressures because they want to become members of a heroin-using group, either of older, more experienced users or of their own peers. Fiddle (1967) focused on the symbiotic relationship between the older addict and the younger initiate. The older addict provides the novice with heroin, paraphernalia for administering it, and instructions in its use as well as the other related knowledge (obtaining drugs, learning criminal skills, etc.) necessary for survival on the streets. In return, the novice provides money and drugs which the more experienced addict needs. Hendler and Stephens (1977) also describe the role of the older addict as being important:

Over half of the sample reported that social acceptance was the primary reason for their first use of narcotics. Some of these individuals reported examples of direct peer pressure in the situation of first use while the majority expressed a desire to become part of the "in crowd." This was especially apparent in individuals who began their use of narcotics at an early age. They often looked up to the older crowd and tried to emulate their behavior. As one young respondent put it, "I just wanted to be part of the crowd. I used to see the older group getting high and getting over with the girls" (Hendler and Stephens, 1977: 30)

While desire to belong to an older, prestigious group is certainly an important reason for some youth turning to the use of heroin, at least one study (Stephens and McBride, 1976) suggested that most youths, prior to their own use of narcotics, either disliked or were indifferent to the addicts in their own neighborhoods. A more important reason for these youths' experimentation with heroin was to gain status within their own nonusing peer group. Feldman (1968) has offered a fascinating explanation for this phenomenon arguing that nonusing adolescent street gang members turn to heroin *because* it is a potent and dangerous drug. The "stand-up cats" or "crazies", as Feldman has variously referred to them, gain status within their own group by facing down all dangers. Usually, they are the strongest, most fearless members of the gang, and their high status within the group depends on these qualities. As further demonstration of their physical and psychic strength, they may use heroin to prove that they can stand up even to the challenge of the potentially serious dangers of heroin use.

Curiosity also plays an important role in why persons first use heroin. It is probably not surprising that in the modern American ghetto (and elsewhere as well) a phenomenon such as heroin use would arouse much curiosity among youth. Heroin use is an important, omnipresent subcultural artifact, which Hanson, et al. (1985) described as being surrounded by an aura of mystery, danger, and status.

Overall, when one examines the reasons for first use, two patterns appear. Some youngsters look up to the older addict and wish to become part of an already well developed heroin-using group; they manifest anticipatory socialization. That is, they set their sights early on a career as a street addict and are in active pursuit of it. Others—probably the majority—first use heroin because of peer pressure and curiosity. They are less likely to be initially seduced by the heroin subcultural life style, per se. Their careers as addicts begin in a much more indirect way.

Circumstances of First Use

Further evidence of these two pathways into heroin addiction is provided by research into events immediately surrounding first use of narcotics. When asked to describe the circumstances of their first use—where they were and with whom—most addicts report first use as occurring in social circumstances. Studies of first use (Stephens and McBride, 1976; Hendler and Stephens, 1977; Waldorf, 1973) all support the hypothesis that narcotics are first used with other persons. Large majorities of subjects are initiated by close friends and acquaintances; it is the rare individual who is "turned on" by a stranger (Crawford, Washington, and Senay, 1983; Gibbons, et al., 1981; Maddux and Desmond, 1981; Hanson, et al., 1985). Interestingly, two studies (Hendler and Stephens, 1977; Stephens and McBride, 1976) point out the largely accidental nature of the first use situation for many subjects. In both studies, almost three-fourths of the respondents said that they had not planned to use narcotics when they found themselves in situations which eventually led to use. For instance, one respondent said:

> I went out to a bar with a friend and left the bar with two other men and women and went to the mens' place. They were just people my friend had met. I hadn't. I didn't know what we were going to the guy's place for. Just something to do. They brought out the stuff, needles equipment, and heroin and everything else and started using. They urged me to use it too. (Stephens and McBride, 1976: 89).

Stephens and McBride further explored the accidental nature of much first use:

The fortuitous nature of the first use situation does not mean that the individual had never had a prior chance to use narcotics; many youths counted addicts among their friends or acquaintances and had previous opportunities to use narcotics. Rather, the first use situation was not planned and the respondents could not recall anything unique or especially noteworthy about the circumstances which led to their first use of narcotics. (Stephens and McBride, 1976: 89)

These data, too, support the idea that for many addicts, the first encounter with heroin appears to be quite "innocent." It is likely that only those who aspire to be addicts deliberately seek out situations in which they can first use narcotics. For the others—who eventually do become addicts—a "drift" hypotheses might be more likely. That is, heroin is available in their neighborhoods, and they simply drift into using it as the appropriate thing to do in certain circumstances.[2]

However they first come to use, the data (Hendler and Stephens, 1977; Crawford, Washington, and Senay, 1983; Stephens and McBride, 1976) show that a variety of narcotics and techniques for administering them are used in the first use situation. Stephens and McBride (1976) indicate that in over three-fourths of the cases, heroin was the first narcotic used. Other narcotics included morphine, cough syrups, paregoric, and methadone. Fifty-eight percent of the respondents used the intravenous route of administration while another 25 percent "snorted" (sniffed).[3] Most others took narcotics orally.

Persons who experiment with heroin are not usually drug-naive. Studies (Waldorf, 1973; Hendler and Stephens, 1977; Weppner and Agar, 1971) document the fact that heroin users had used marihuana and alcohol before they had ever tried heroin or other narcotics. Much smaller percentages had some experience with glue sniffing, barbiturates, amphetamines, LSD, and cocaine.

One interesting aspect of the first use situation is the person's physiological and psychological reaction to heroin. Various studies have shown that a quarter to over three-fourths of neophyte users report euphoria on first use. However, large percentages of experimenters experience nausea and vomiting upon first use (Hendler and Stephens, 1977; Crawford, Washington, and Senay, 1983; Maddux and Desmond, 1981; Hanson, et al., 1985). McAuliffe (1975) reports that three-fourths of the addicts he studied vomited on first use of a narcotic. The intriguing question is: Why would such individuals try narcotics again if they had such a negative experience? In exploring this question, McAuliffe (1975) discovers a number of reasons for continued use. First, the negative effects of nausea and vomiting usually occur only in the first few instances of use. Second, the vomiting is often described as not being that unpleasant; possibly this reaction is a result of the analgesic effects of the heroin. Third, many persons who continue use report they were forewarned about possible vomiting the first few times and were assured these effects would eventually disappear. Fourth, the neophytes often had the support of their heroin-using group. The desire to belong, as I have already suggested, is a potent force, not only in encouraging first use, but in bolstering the resolve of the neophyte to use again despite initial unpleasant effects. Finally, the negative effects of the heroin are often overwhelmed by the euphoria which emerges, even in these first use instances. Hendler and Stephens report such effects:

> I threw up. I was sick, real sick. First I felt like I was gonna faint. Then I threw up and after I threw up I felt more relieved and relaxed. I felt like I was on a cloud. I felt down. Like there was no worries. I wasn't tired and I just sat there and wanted to nod.
>
> It took a little while to affect me. It was like a real groggy feeling...everything groggy...your eyes heavy and your stomach flips. Your stomach seems like it's rotating, it's floating in your belly. Your throat is dry. You feel real relaxed, extra comfortable. (Hendler and Stephens, 1977).

This feeling of euphoria remains a constant. Experienced addicts, when asked to describe the feelings imported by heroin, most often utilize the words *pleasure* and *relaxation*.

What we see, then, is a confluence of elements which together create the first use situation. There is the opportunity to use, the availability of the drug, the willingness of the person to use on that occasion, and the social milieu supportive of such use. While some persons deliberately seek out situations conducive to first use, most stumble upon them quite accidentally.

The Importance of the First Few Drug Use Instances

TABLE 6
REASONS FOR CONTINUING OR DISCONTINUING OPIATE USE
BEYOND THE FIRST DOSE (JOHNS HOPKINS STUDY)

ADDICTS' REASONS FOR CONTINUING OPIATE USE FOLLOWING "SICK" OR "SICK AND GOOD" REACTION	FREQUENCY*	NONADDICTS' REASONS FOR DISCONTINUING OPIATE USE AFTER TRYING IT ONCE OR TWICE ONLY	FREQUENCY**
Got sick, but also got high. I liked high so much, did it again in spite of the sickness.	22	Got sick	25
		Did not like the high	7
Sickness not like normal sickness. Just threw up, but not painfully sick.	7	Did not like drug experience	4
Friends forewarned him or explained that sickness was common first reaction which would pass, and encouraged him to try again.	11	Had job, family, responsibilities	4
		Did not want to get involved in addict life	3
Everyone else was getting high. It must have been something about him or something else besides the drug. So, tried it again to see if he too could get high.	10	Not worth expense	3
		Got hepatitis	3
		Overdosed	2
Wanted to be like everyone else and part of the crowd, so tried again.	3	Needle shy	2

*Some respondents gave more than one reason. The maximum possible frequency for each reason was 44.

** The maximum possible frequency for each reason was 49. Mentioned by only one respondent were: fear of addiction, went into army, got arrested, afraid of what people would say, and wanted to avoid the long-term effects of drugs.

Source: McAuliffe, 1975.

The first few encounters with narcotics seem to be crucial in determining whether a person continues to use them. McAuliffe (1975) presented data (see Table 6) which differentiate those who continue to use from those who eschew further use of narcotics. Those who persevere find both personal and social rewards in continued use. While they may have had some negative experiences with initial use, they negate these effects and continue to use. Notice that for those who continue, the sickness is minimized either by the effects of the high or because illness was an expected consequence of initial use. Note also the importance of the group both in defining the effects of the drug and in encouraging subsequent use.[4] For those who discontinue use, however, the single most important reason for forswearing future use is the experience of becoming sick. Some of the other reasons for discontinuing use ("did not like high" or "did not like drug experience") are related to the unpleasant effects of the drug, as well.

Other researchers also have discussed the importance of the user's subjective interpretation of the first use experience. In contrasting moderate and light users with addicts and heavy experimenters, Crawford, et al. (1983) reported differences in these groups' initial experiences with heroin. Those who become heavier users more frequently report liking "the high" on initial use. They like the "nod," the feeling of relaxation and the freedom from worry, whereas more moderate users emphasize relaxation and the sociable experience of using with others. Haertzer, Kocher, and Miyasato (1983) strongly linked liking the drug on first use to subsequent habitual use.

One study focused on the second use situation of addicts (Hendler and Stephens, 1977). Second use occurs within a very short period of time; usually within one week. Those who have the most negative experiences on first use generally wait the longest. Use, as in the initial encounter with heroin, is almost always in the company of others. Two-fifths of the respondents say they used again because they enjoyed the high they experienced sometime during the first use. A third say that social acceptance is the reason for second use. Few of the respondents report continuing negative physical effects associated with continued use of narcotics. Additionally, a whole network of social interaction effects are important to continuing drug use beyond the first few times.

Another factor which must be considered in determining the rewarding or punishing effect of narcotics use is the social situation that follows the use of the drug. In several cases, respondents reported having sex after their first or second experience with narcotics. Others reported going to or being in a party situation at the time of their first two experiences with narcotics. Many report being more talkative and more able to "rap to the girls", yet others report just sitting around, nodding, or watching television as their only activities after use. Some report verbal reinforcement of their behavior by their friends after narcotics use, yet others report negative social contacts with nondrug using peers. Although no clear-cut relationship exists between activities that follow initial and secondary experiences with narcotics and rapidity of involvement in the addict subculture, it appears that for many individuals the nature of such post-narcotic use activities were of major importance in motivating them to become more heavily involved with narcotics. (Hendler and Stephens, 1977: 32)

The Honeymoon Period

The honeymoon period begins for users when they first experience euphoria uncomplicated by any negative physical side effects and ceases when they realize that, like all good things, "this high without penalties" period must end. This realization usually occurs when addicts first discover they are physiologically addicted. The honeymoon often lasts for most addicts about the same length of time the honeymoon endures in the more traditional sense of the term—from six to twelve months (Hendler and Stephens, 1977; Stephens and McBride, 1976; Maddux and Desmond, 1981). The honeymoon is typically at least six months shorter for females than males (Anglin, 1987). Usually addicts come to use more narcotics with greater frequency during this period. Almost always there is a shift to heroin use if heroin was not the first narcotic taken. Honeymooners almost always move to intravenous injection if this route was not initially used.[5] While marihuana and other drugs often are still used, heroin begins to assume a previously unexperienced prominence. Drugs such as marihuana and cocaine are usually no longer solely used for their own effects but rather are used to enhance the effects of the heroin "high" (Hendler and Stephens, 1977).

Other important changes are beginning to take place in the honeymooners' lives—especially in regard to their activities and their relationships with family, friends and addicts. Only small proportions of subjects report that their parents are aware of their narcotics use (Hendler and Stephens, 1977). For those who are discovered, life at home becomes less tolerable. Users are pressured to discontinue use and, when they do not, hostility flares— sometimes to the point of the user being ejected from home. Honeymooners' reactions to warnings about the dangers of drug use are defensive and argumentative, and they insist on their right to "do their own thing." Users begin more and more to manipulate parents and friends and increasingly to sever ties with more conventional societal contacts. Students drop out of school, and tardiness and other problems at work, related to heroin use, escalate (Hendler and Stephens, 1977).

While involvement in crime remains relatively low for some, there is nevertheless a trend towards increased criminality to finance drug use, especially amongst those whose use patterns become heavier. "Seventy percent of those who had not reported criminal involvement prior to their first narcotics use, however, were to some extent supporting their narcotics use through illegal sources prior to their addiction to the drug" (Hendler and Stephens, 1977: 35).

Neophyte heroin users usually think positively about the honeymoon period. While problems related to drug use begin to appear, they are not so prominent as to be really disruptive in the neophytes' lives. When asked why they continue to use narcotics during this period, honeymooners cite reasons related to the quality of the euphoric high, their desire to remain part of the "in crowd," and the excitement of the drug life—especially surrounding the purchase and, at times, profitable reselling of drugs. The negative aspects of the life have not yet impinged in any meaningful way on their lives. The unpleasant consequences—risk of arrest, danger of overdosing, and the sickness of withdrawal—often known through the example provided by others on the scene, are discounted. This risk discounting process, discussed in detail by Fiddle (1969), generally rests upon the neophytes' feeling of omnipotence regarding their drug use. They feel that they are either too skillful to allow any of these negative things to happen to them or that, at any rate, these dangers are all part of the exciting street scene. Finally, they reason that if by chance any of the above misfortunes were to befall them, they would be able to live through the experience and no great or lasting harm would come to them. As Hendler and Stephens (1977) point out, only one of their thirty subjects perceived that heroin use was a real problem during this honeymoon period.

First Addiction

Finally, after a period of regular use, there comes a point when honeymooners realize that they are physically addicted. Typically, such realization is indirect; the user wakes one morning with a case of the "flu" which quickly disappears with the next shot. Often less than half recognize these classical withdrawal symptoms (Hendler and Stephens, 1977). The rest rely upon friends to correctly identify the source of their physical distress[6]. Despite this recognition, only about a quarter make attempts to cease use of narcotics. While about a third report being frightened by the turn of events, they resolve to continue use. A fifth actually are happy to be finally addicted:

> I felt good about it. Everybody glorified being sick; I felt big being strung out.
>   It was like a big thing bein' hooked. Wow, I didn't really know what hooked meant. I just thought 'Now, I'm part of the crowd.' (Hendler and Stephens, 1977: 41)

These reactions provide another point of differentiation between those who continue to use narcotics and those who halt use. In other words, first addiction, another crucial step in the process of becoming a street addict, is one that only some of the neophyte users decide to take. One intriguing study of cessation patterns among neophyte heroin users was conducted by Schasre (1966). He contrasted two groups of heroin users—those who ceased use for a specific reason and those who stopped but without specifically deciding to do so. The results of his study are presented in Table 7.

TABLE 7

CESSATION OF DRUG USE WITH AND WITHOUT A SPECIFIC
DECISION TO STOP DRUG USE

SIGNIFICANT FACTOR CESSATION FOLLOWING SPECIFIC DECISION	NO. OF CASES	SIGNIFICANT FACTOR WITHOUT SPECIFIC DECISION	NO. OF CASES
Experienced Physical Addiction	9	Supplier Arrested	9
Friends Convicted on Narcotics Charges	4	Ex-User Moved from Neighborhood	6
Subject Arrested for Marks	2	Ex-User Moved from Town	3
Pressure From Girl Friend	2	Supplier Lost His Heroin Source	3
Friend Died of Heroin Overdose	1	Supplier Moved from Town	1
TOTAL	18		22

Adopted from Schasre, 1966.

As one can see from the table, these two groups are markedly different. Those who specifically decide to give up heroin use do so primarily because they are afraid of the physiological and social consequences. In other words, the risks of heroin use—physical addiction, overdose, and arrest—which are discounted by those who continue to use, are frightening enough to others to cause them to cease use. Those who stop using without a specific reason do so for what we might call "ecological" or "environmental" reasons. That is, they either move away from drug sources or lose their drug source (i.e. supplier). Interestingly, Schasre (1966) reports that eleven of those thirteen people who lost their supply of heroin made immediate unsuccessful attempts to locate other sources of drugs.

There are data which somewhat corroborate Schasre's findings (Brown et al., 1971). Separate sample of adult males, adult females, and juvenile males who ultimately remained street addicts were asked to relate their reasons for quitting use of heroin the first time. For all three groups, the two major reasons stated were "drug related physical problems" and "effort to change life pattern." Other major responses were: "drug related family problems," "expense," and, for the juveniles, "influence of friends" and "concern about punishment for illegal acts." While all of these persons returned to heroin use, there is an interesting parallel with those in Schasre's (1966) study who made a deliberate attempt to cease use. Both groups were concerned about physiological dangers, and they did not want to become entangled in the many problems presented by the drug way of life.

What these data as a whole demonstrate is the increasing commitment to the street addict role as one moves from experimenter to full-fledged addict. Clearly, throughout this process, there are those for whom the street addict role identity is not appropriate (that is, incongruent with their desired selves and current roles), and they either continue to use occasionally or forego the further use of heroin. For many, however, the street addict role identity "fits," and they become ever more enmeshed in the subculture.

This process of increasing involvement in a deviant life style has been analyzed by Lemert (1951) and was described in Chapter 2. Basically, the individual comes to think of him or her self more and more as a deviant, partially as the result of labelling by others. He or she becomes estranged from nondeviant others, and this leads to a spiraling process of further self identification as a deviant.[7] This process is what essentially happens to the neophyte once he or she becomes addicted and makes the decision, either consciously or unconsciously, to commit him or her self to becoming a street addict. In one study addicts were asked to re-create retrospectively their lives at three points: right before they first used narcotics, right when they first used narcotics, and when they first realized they were addicted (Stephens and McBride, 1976). There is increased estrangement from conventional activities as addicts become more involved with narcotics. Addicts interact more intensely with other members of the addict subculture, while at the same time avoiding family and nonaddict friends. A complementary process is taking place; family and friends begin to avoid the addict. Participation in criminal activities rises dramatically, while there are marked decreases in more conventional activities (work or school). Thus, at the point of addiction, junkies become existentially more committed to thinking of themselves as street addicts and behaving as such. Labelling by others helps to further confirm their new identities. These processes of isolation and closure lead to further commitment to the street addict role.

Life as a Junkie

Once addicts become immersed in the subculture, two major events dominate their lives. One is *copping*—the search for heroin. The other is *hustling*—the often illegal quest for the money to purchase drugs and to provide living expenses. Large portions of the street addict's day are filled with these two events.

Copping

Copping, although a complex and important event in the addict lifestyle, has not received very much attention in the literature. An exception is Agar (1973), who focused on copping in his linguistic analysis of the street life. He emphasized the bargaining behavior that occurs between the dealer, who wants to maximize profits, and the junkies, who want to maximize the quality and amount of heroin they receive. An intrinsic part of copping, as Agar (1973) points out, is avoidance of the "burn"—purchase of bags which either contain inferior heroin or no heroin at all.

One study "Copping and Caveat Emptor: The Street Addict as Consumer," examined the drug purchase transaction in some detail (Stephens and Smith, 1976). It views copping as a sequential process which includes finding the best heroin while avoiding the burn. A number of strategies are employed by addicts to find the best heroin. By far, the most frequently used technique is to utilize the same dealer or dealers over time. Hopefully, an element of some trust is built up between the customer and the illegal merchant so that the regular customer expects to be treated "right." Another strategy is to shop around for the highest quality drugs.

This is accomplished in one of three ways. First, one frequents certain copping areas in the city such as Harlem, in New York, where the heroin is better and cheaper than in more remote sites such as the copping areas of Queens. Secondly, one uses the "wire," or junkie gossip and information network, to find out which dealers are carrying the best stuff. Finally, if all else fails, one uses a "steerer" to direct one to the best heroin.

The burn is an omnipresent danger in the street addict world. A number of strategies are employed to avoid it. One technique, albeit an infrequently used one, is "tasting." In tasting, the addict injects a small quantity of the proffered heroin to ascertain its quality. This is not only an unreliable technique but is infrequently used because both buyer and seller want to transact business as quickly and as inconspicuously as possible. Two more popular techniques for avoiding the burn are buying from "trusted" dealers and "holding the seller responsible." As we already noted, buying from a regular dealer minimizes, but certainly does not eliminate, the chance that one will get burned. If one has the appropriate reputation and physical and psychological qualities, one can also let the dealers know that they will be "held responsible" if one is burned. Yet another way of avoiding the burn is to "play it cool" at all times. Junkies who are playing it cool do not let a dealer know that they are "sick." By masking withdrawal symptoms, they are less likely to be rushed into buying inferior drugs. Avoiding the burn is also possible if one is able to intercept a dealer immediately after his wholesale purchase of heroin. The dealer will not have had the opportunity to return to his crib and "cut" the heroin (that is, add diluents such as quinine or lactose to the heroin), and thus a higher quality purchase is assured.

Addicts have a number of recourses if they are burned (Stephens and Smith, 1976). First, they can simply discontinue their relationship with that particular dealer. Or they can demand recompense—again, a strategy which is more effective if one is physically able to carry out threats or if the dealer is caught in an embarrassing public situation. Finally, the junkie can retaliate against the dealer; such retaliation ranges all the way from "bad-mouthing the dealer on the wire" to informing to the police.

However they come to cop drugs, the evidence is clear that street addicts use enormous quantities of drugs. Johnson, et al. (1985) reported that dollar values of drugs used per year are estimated to be: for the irregular user, $5,186 worth of drugs, with $1,389 of this amount going for heroin; for the regular user, the figures are $9,847 and $6,431 respectively; and for the daily user the amounts are $17,283, with $13,189 being spent on heroin[8] (Johnson et al., 1985). Maddux and Desmond (1981) estimated that their heroin users consumed an average annual retail amount of $7,064. It is no surprise that many addicts must turn to crime in order to support such lavish drug consumption patterns.

Hustling

The subject of criminality among addicts has probably spawned more studies than any other issue in the field of drug use. It would be impossible in this limited space to review these many studies. Some relatively recent studies do a good job of summarizing the literature (Inciardi, 1981; Gandossy, et al., 1980). Instead, in this section, I shall focus on the extent and types of criminal activity common among addicts. Then I shall deal with what probably is the single most important topic in this research: the relationship between hustling and copping.

Types of Crimes Committed

From studies based on both arrest statistics and self-reports, it is well established that addicts commit a large variety of crimes (Gandossy, et al., 1980; Voss and Stephens, 1973; Inciardi, 1981; Johnson, et al., 1985). However, it is also true that addicts do not commit all types of crime with the same regularity. The chief motivation for almost all addict crime is the production of income. As proof of this statement, one need only look at a recently produced typology of addicts based on the type and extent of criminal activity (Shaffer, Nurco, and Kinlock, 1984). Using a clustering technique for a sample of addicted street addicts, the researchers found the types indicated in Figure 1.

FIGURE 1

PERCENT OF ADDICTS		TYPE
33.1	I	Marginal Criminals*
20.3	II	Drug Dealers
20.6	III	Thieves
13.8	IV	Illegal Gamblers
5.4	V	Con Men (forgery and con games)
3.4	VI	Violent (violence and theft)
2.0	VII	Super Con Men (more con games than V)
1.4	VIII	Super Violent (more violent than VI)

* Less criminally involved than other types but when involved committed mostly theft, drug dealing and gambling offenses.

The typology[9] in Figure 1 succinctly summarizes several major points about addicts' criminality. It illustrates the wide variety of crimes committed by addicts. It also supports the point made previously about addict crime being primarily income oriented. Note also that only small percentages of addicts (4.8 percent) specialize in violent activities as a means of acquiring money.[10] Drug sales emerge as an important source of income. Not only do these crimes involve the direct sales of drugs, but they include a host of other drug distribution activities which yield either income or drugs to the addict. Included here are "touts" (persons who are paid to spread the word that certain dealers have good stuff), "cop men" (persons who buy drugs for other users), "holders" (persons who physically hold heroin for a dealer), "resource providers" (shooting gallery operators and persons who rent drug injection paraphernalia), and "testers" (persons who assess the quality of a particular batch of heroin). Clearly, addicts use a wide variety of hustling activities in order to come by the money needed to support their habit.

Amount of Crime

However they hustle, addicts are responsible for enormous amounts of crime. In fact, several recent studies indicate that the large amount of crime borders on the unbelievable. One of these studies (Ball, Shaffer, and Nurco, 1983) is summarized in Table 8.

TABLE 8
TOTAL CRIME-DAYS FOR THEFT, VIOLENCE, DEALING, CONFIDENCE, AND
OTHER OFFENSES FOR 354 MALE ADDICTS

TYPE OF CRIME-DAYS	NO. OF CRIME-DAYS	MEAN CRIME-DAYS PER ADDICT	% CRIME-DAYS OF EACH TYPE
1. Theft of property	293,308	8286	37.9
2. Violent offenses	16,316	461	2.1
3. Drug Sales	205,692	5811	26.5
4. Confidence, forgery, etc.	60,882	1720	7.9
5. Other offenses	198,579	5610	25.6
Total crime-days	774,777	2188	

From Ball, Shaffer, and Nurco, 1983: 125.

Table 8 indicates that over a nine year period when 354 addicts were "at risk" (that is, free on the streets), they committed crimes on a total of 774,777 days (each such day on which a crime was committed was defined as a crime day). The mean number of crime days was 2,188.6 for the nine year period. This averages out to about 255 days of crime per year per addict. Further, addicts engaged in two or more different types of crime on any one day for about one third of the years they were addicted. Interestingly, less than one percent of all the crimes committed by these addicts resulted in an arrest.

Johnson, et al. (1985) conducted a massive, in-depth study of the economic behavior of addicts. While the findings of the study are too numerous and complex to summarize here easily, some of the findings most relevant to the present discussion are:

1) Regular users[11] committed 985 crimes per year while daily users engaged in 1,089 crimes per year. The figure for irregular heroin users was 360 per year. These figures do not include minor crimes and miscellaneous drug crimes (such as theft of drugs from dealers). If these were included, daily users committed more than 1,400 crimes per year (or almost 3.8 per day.) Regular users committed more than 1,200 per year, and irregular users more than 500 per year.

2) Daily heroin users committed 209 non-drug crimes (all crimes unrelated to drug sales and distributional activities) per year compared with 162 for regular users and 116 for irregular users. Drug business crime (drug sales, "steering," etc.) equalled 245 per year for irregular users, 823 for regular users, and 840 for daily users.

3) The annualized income from all crime (both drug and non-drug) was over $18,000, $11,000 of which was in actual cash income. The rest was the value of drugs received in payment for some drug distributional activity (sales, touting, etc.). Figures for regular users were $11,203 and $7,121, and for irregular users were $6,004 and $4,451 respectively.

4) Daily users, on the average, distribute drugs worth about $20,000 per year through STC (Steering, touting and copping): "steering" (directing a potential customer to a dealer, "touting" (finding customers for a particular dealer) and "copping" (buying drugs from a dealer for a customer). Another $6,000 worth of drugs per year are distributed through direct sales by daily users. Total value of drugs distributed through STC or sales for regular users was $14,260 and $4,927 for irregular users.

In short, Johnson, et al. (1985) found that the amounts of crime committed varied among the three types of users, with more crimes (and more serious crimes) being associated with more extensive use of heroin. In fact, at the aggregate level for all users, these researchers found that noncriminal income (of which we will speak later in this chapter) about equalled non-drug expenditures and criminal income approximately equalled the actual annual consumption of drugs. In a nutshell, these findings indicate that amount of crime committed is related in a very direct way to amount of drugs consumed.

Johnson, et al. (1985) attempted to assess the overall negative economic consequences of the addict lifestyle. They developed a composite measure called the "annualized economic consequences of heroin abusers' lifestyle." While the operationalization of this variable is too complicated to detail here (see Johnson, et al., 1985: 104–114), it is principally concerned with "assigning dollar amounts to criminal activity and other aspects of the heroin abuser's lifestyle" including avoided expenditures such as free drugs, free meals and lodging, tax evasion, and loans from relatives and friends (Johnson, et al., 1985: 104). Note carefully that the measure does not include either the cost of public response to crime (such as criminal justice costs) or private reactions to the addict lifestyle (private security guards, etc.). Nor does it include the loss to the economy due to unemployment (forgone productivity). Using this measure, then, Johnson, et al. (1985) estimate the annualized economic consequences to be $15,033 for the irregular user, $32,672 for the regular user, and an astounding $55,455 for the daily user. Truly, we can say that heroin use has a profound economic and social impact on our society.

The Relationship Between "Copping" and "Hustling"

These findings are very important to understanding the relationship between drug use and criminality. The issue can be couched in two different questions. First, do most persons commit crime before they first use narcotics, or are they criminal after they become acquainted with narcotics? Second, what is the relationship between the amount of drugs consumed and the extent of criminality?

Regarding the first question, the evidence is not totally clear. Partially, this is due to methodological problems. (For a discussion of these problems, see Stephens and Levine [1973], Gandossy, et al. [1980], and Pottieger [1981].) Basically, despite these methodological problems, I think some major conclusions can be drawn. Most persons probably are neither arrested nor commit serious crimes before they first use any psychoactive substance (if this includes alcohol or marijuana). Larger percentages of the population commit crimes and are arrested after they first use marijuana (which almost always precedes narcotics use) but before they first use narcotics. After they begin to regularly use narcotics, much larger percentages of the population begin to commit crime[12] (Voss and Stephens, 1973; O'Donnell, 1969; Gandossy, et al., 1980). In this sense, then, initial and increasing involvement with heroin leads to an increase in criminality. But it does not appear to be true that heroin "leads to" or "forces" otherwise innocent youth into a life of crime. In fact, I believe a good perspective on this issue is provided by Joel Fort who concluded:

A number of "chicken and egg" studies have been done as to whether addicts were criminal before or after becoming addicted. The overall results appear to indicate that most illegal narcotics users in the United States have grown up in environments generally conducive to delinquency and crime, and the drug subculture can become for some a part of a broader criminal life style. (Fort, 1969: 115)

Once the user becomes heavily involved with narcotics, however, the relationship between amount of use and extent of criminality becomes much clearer. Addicts commit much more crime in periods when they are addicted (Ball, Shaffer, and Nurco, 1983). A 75 percent decrease in crime is observed when the first drug-free period subsequent to addiction was contrasted with the first addiction period. There is a remarkable degree of stability in terms of the frequency of criminal behavior for all the periods during which the subjects were addicted. "The most parsimonious explanation of these consistent changes in crime rates is that heroin addiction contributes to, or causes, an increase in crime" (Ball, Shaffer, and Nurco, 1983: 140). Johnson, et al. (1985), whose work was cited previously, provides corroboration for this conclusion. For, as we saw in their conclusions, both the incidence and seriousness of crime increases with greater heroin use.

We have focused on studies which relate statistically the size of one's "habit" to one's "hustling" activity. One study (Smith and Stephens, 1976) attempted to view this issue at the experiential level of the individual junkie. Thirty addicts were asked to describe "hustling" and "copping" activities for the same period of time. Smith and Stephens (1976) discovered three major patterns of relationships between size of "score" (in terms of dollars obtained from a criminal activity) and amount of drugs consumed. The three patterns, shown in Figure 2, reveal a strong relationship between "copping" and "hustling." Ordinarily, addicts will score an average number of dollars, buy and use an average amount of heroin and other drugs, and will likely go out on the streets again to engage in a criminal hustle. However, when they score big, they buy more than an average amount of drugs and then "rest" (refrain from "hustling") for a day or two. Conversely, if they score little or no money, they consume a lower than average amount of drugs, thereby compelling them to "hustle" further. These three patterns were observed among a majority of the addicts studied. Yet a number of other patterns were observed, as well.

FIGURE 2

"SCORE"	DRUG USE	LIKELIHOOD OF CRIMINAL ACTIVITY
Average	Average	Average
High	High	Low or none
Low	Low or average	Average

In analyzing why so many other patterns occurred, Smith and Stephens (1976) found a number of confounding factors. These factors demonstrate the richness of experiences and uncertainties which contribute to the excitement of the street life. The confounding factors were divided into those which were principally environmental, motivational, or related to the addict's skill level. The first of these environmental factors is labelled "cyclical events," and usually is related to the day of the week that a certain hustling activity is most likely to pay off. Pimps, on one hand, look forward to weekends when their women are most in demand. Shoplifters, on the other hand, dread Sundays, when many stores are closed. A second confounding factor is the purely accidental event— a burglar is interrupted by the arrival of the homeowner, or heroin cannot be "copped" because of police "heat" in the "copping area." A third environmental factor is the availability of supplemental income to the addict from friends and relatives; such additional income might influence the amount of drugs purchased or the need to hustle. Another factor is the relationship the addict has with other people on the scene, especially the relationship with a dealer who might extend credit on a particularly poor "hustling" day. The final environmental confounding factor is the law enforcement patterns which might influence the availability of drugs on the street or the addict's ability to ply his or her criminal trade.

The second major category of confounding factors is motivational —it relates to addicts' reasons for using drugs and being in the drug life. It includes such factors as their willingness and ability to use other drugs (such as methadone) to stave off withdrawal should heroin be scarce. Another motivational confounding factor is the addicts' need for additional funds to support themselves and their families. Yet another motivational factor is their psychopharmacological state. If they are beginning to undergo serious withdrawal, there is a very high likelihood that they will go out and hustle (and probably take more chances than they ordinarily would.) The final motivational confounding factor is their commitment to the street addict lifestyle. Those most committed to the lifestyle are most likely to engage in prolonged hustling and drug taking.

The third set of confounding factors is related to the addicts' skill level. The more skillful criminals will have more stable incomes. Those with regular illegal occupations, such as numbers runners, are more likely to have stable "hustling-copping" patterns. Conversely, those with no criminal skills—the "flatfooted hustlers"—will have more unstable patterns.

These hustling-copping patterns I have described and the confounding factors which help to influence them demonstrate the complex kinds of situations addicts encounter on the street. They also illustrate the day to day life of persons once they become committed to the street addict life.

Employment Patterns of Street Addicts

The extent to which addicts are able to support themselves through legitimate employment is still something of an open question. Partially, this is the result of sampling problems encountered by the various studies which have explored this issue. For instance, Caplovitz (1976) studied addicts who held full-time jobs while they were addicted. The addicts studied by Johnson, et al. (1985) included mostly street people, and this sample was probably less likely to include persons employed full-time. Consequently, one would conclude from Caplovitz's work (1976) that many addicts can maintain full-time employment while the conclusions of Johnson, et al. (1985) would not be as sanguine.

Caplovitz (1976) studied 555 addicts enrolled in New York City treatment programs who held full-time jobs for at least three months while they were addicted.[13] Almost a third had held full-time jobs for a minimum of three years and 70 percent had held a full-time job for a year while they were addicted. In comparing these working addicts with unemployed addicts, he found that working addicts were more similar demographically to the general population in more respects[14] than the nonworking addicts. Caplovitz (1976) also developed scales to measure the extent of drug involvement and the negative impact of drugs on work. As might be expected, the greater the involvement with drugs, the greater the negative impact on the job situation. Interestingly though, almost two-thirds of the addicts reported that both they and their supervisors felt they were doing a very good job. Caplovitz (1976) also noted that a majority of the subjects resorted to crime in order to supplement their legitimate income; about a third reported stealing from their employers.

Other data (Nurco and Lerner, 1974) corroborate Caplovitz's (1976) finding that addicts, to some extent, are capable of holding jobs. Unemployment actually decreases after one has become addicted. However, this partly is due to the low age of first addiction; the subjects were too young to have had a job before their first addiction. Two-thirds of the subjects indicated that their longest held post-addiction job was twelve months or less. However, as their habit grows, it becomes more expensive, and legitimate income is no longer sufficient to support it. Addicts increasingly turn to crime and either quit or are fired. Some addicts stay on jobs specifically because it gives them the opportunity to steal goods which can later be sold (Nurco and Lerner, 1974).

Maddux and Desmond, (1981) report that during the first decade after initial drug use, their subjects were employed an average of 62 percent of the time (when they were free on the streets). In the second decade, the average employment rate was 58 percent. Both of these figures include part-time employment; at no time did the proportion of subjects employed full-time greatly exceed 50 percent (Maddux and Desmond, 1981).

Johnson, et al. (1985) found even lower employment figures. Their subjects were employed only about 6 percent of the time. Most of this employment consisted of short-term odd jobs—helping friends move, washing cars, painting apartments, etc.—and these activities provided only about $1,000 per year out of a total average income of approximately $17,000. As one might expect, the greater the involvement with heroin, the lower the relative percentage of total income accounted for by legitimate employment.

As we saw in the previous chapter, most heroin users who were marginal to both the subculture and the larger society worked legitimate jobs at least occasionally (Hanson, et al., 1985). About one-fourth of them reported legitimate employment as their main source of income. It would appear for most of these heroin users, however, that sporadic legitimate employment is just one other "hustle" which they use to obtain money. This is probably to be expected, given low employment rates of ghetto dwellers in general and the low-paying jobs available to those who are fortunate enough to find employment at all.

In the final analysis, what we find is that as persons become enmeshed in the street addict lifestyle, they increasingly use a strategy which has been described by Goldstein (1981) as "getting over." Not only do junkies engage in predatory crime (robbery, burglary, etc.), but they also receive income from a mixture of nonpredatory crime, legitimate employment, public support, contributions from friends and/or family, and miscellaneous "hustling" (including bartering). The world of the street addict is a catch-as-catch-can melange of activities designed first to assure an adequate supply of money for drugs and secondly to provide for all other living expenses. In addition to hustling, addicts borrow money from friends, sell methadone doses, live with and accept meals from family, paramours, and friends, and in general do whatever is necessary to "take care of business." Most of the addict's income will come from crime. In fact, Johnson, et al. (1985) estimate that on the average about $12,000 out of a total annualized income of $17,000 for heroin users comes from criminal activities. The rest comes from other sources addicts use to keep body and soul together.

Other Aspects of the Life

Life as an addict does not consist merely of "hustling" and "copping." It is filled with myriad other activities and risks. In fact, the variety presented by the life is probably one of its chief attractions. In addition to the usual activities of "copping" and "hustling," the addict is also faced with avoiding arrest and incarceration, making decisions about whether and when to enter treatment, and attempting to avoid the hazards to one's health posed by the addict lifestyle. Because of all these factors, the addict does not usually have prolonged "runs" of heroin use. Often such "runs" are punctuated with periods off the streets including incarceration and time spent in treatment centers. As Waldorf noted:

> I observed that most addicts spend a good part of their careers in addiction in jail and that many make occasional but real efforts to abstain from heroin use after incarceration or treatment. An addict may say that he has been addicted for 13 years, but as you delve into his history you may learn that 6 years of that time have been spent in jail, another year in various treatment programs, and, perhaps, 6 months in actual abstention outside of an institution. The actual duration of physical addiction and heroin use is often much shorter and more sporadic than one would expect from the original, superficial report...What many

persons may be describing is not the length of actual physical addiction but the length of time they have considered
themselves addicts—which for many may be more a social
status than a physical condition. (Waldorf, 1973: 410)

In order to illustrate this point further, one need only look at data
provided by Maddux and Desmond (1981).

TABLE 9
MEAN YEARS IN DIFFERENT DRUG-USE STATUSES OF 154 SUBJECTS
DURING 20 CALENDAR YEARS AFTER YEAR OF FIRST OPIOID DRUG USE

| | MEAN YEARS | | |
STATUS	FIRST DECADE	SECOND DECADE	BOTH
Using illicit opioid daily	4.5	3.1	7.6
Using occasionally	1.2	0.4	1.6
Methadone maintenance	0.0	0.7	0.7
Institutionalized	2.3	3.6	5.9
Dead	0.0	0.3	0.3
Abstinent	1.6	1.5	3.1
Status unknown	0.4	0.4	0.8
Total	10.0	10.0	20.0

From Maddux and Desmond, 1981: 94.

Table 9 summarizes the two decade experience of 154 of their
study subjects. As one can see, for 9.2 out of the 20 years, the
subjects were using opioids and for 7.6 of these years they were
using opioids on a daily basis. They were either institutionalized
or in methadone treatment for 6.6 years and were voluntarily
abstinent for only 3.1 years. Thus, for significant portions of their
lives as addicts, they were not hustling and copping but instead
were in treatment or in jail. For only about 16 percent of the time
were they voluntarily abstinent.

One omnipresent danger in the life is death. Most studies have
shown that addicts have high death rates. (For a review of these
studies, see Maddux and Desmond [1981: 178–194].) Maddux
and Desmond (1981) calculate the age-adjusted death rates among

addicts to be from two to four times greater than expected. The chief causes of such deaths are homicide, overdose, accidents, and cirrhosis of the liver. The fact that death is an ever-present player on the scene may indeed lead to the heightened sense of adventure that some addicts feel.

However, as in all things, the adventure and excitement waxes and wanes. In a typical career, the addict often climbs to the heights of ecstasy and self-satisfaction only to plummet to the depths of great despair. At one moment, the junkie is "taking care of business"—leading an exciting, eventful life filled with the rewards of drugs, material possessions, and status among peers. In the next instance, however, the habit becomes unmanageably large and expensive, and the descent to the level of the "greasy dope-fiend" begins. It is often at this stage—when the addict can no longer play the street addict role—(when he suffers role strain or role conflict) that the junkie seeks treatment.[15]

Agar (1971) beautifully illustrates this roller coaster type of life in his analysis of two street addict "toasts," or epic-type poems which depict various aspects of the street life. One such "toast" "Honky Tonk Bud," portrays the junkie who is at the apex of his career—the true "cool cat" who has all the prestige and material possessions he needs. The other "toast," "King Heroin," paints a picture of a down-and-out junkie who has lost control of his life and is dominated and destroyed by heroin.

Leaving the Life

It is when they are in this latter stage that junkies are most likely to think of leaving the life. This process of giving up the street addict role has been studied in some detail, most notably by Charles Winick. In a now classic article, he posited the maturation hypothesis, which he explains as follows:

> Maturing out of addiction is the name we can give to the process by which the addict stops taking drugs, as the problems for which he originally began taking drugs becomes less salient and less urgent, if our hypothesis is

correct. It is as if, metaphorically speaking, the addicts' inner fires have become banked by their thirties. They may feel that less is expected of them in the way of sex, aggressiveness, a vocation, helping their parents, or starting a family. As a result of some process of emotional homeostasis, the stresses and strains of life are becoming sufficiently stabilized for a typical addict in his thirties so that he can face them without the support provided by narcotics. (Winick, 1962: 5)

Winick reached these conclusions through analysis of a now defunct master file of addicts once maintained by the Federal Bureau of Narcotics. Names were regularly fed to the Bureau by federal, state, and local law enforcement and health agencies. If an addict's name which had once appeared on the list was not supplied again to the Bureau within five years, Winick reasoned that this person could be counted as abstinent. (Deaths, Winick argued, would probably be rather randomly distributed over the age categories in which he was interested.) Analyzing these data, Winick found that almost two-thirds of the addicts originally reported were no longer to be found on the list. He further discovered that most of these cases had become inactive in their thirties, and he reasoned that they had matured out of addiction. This process usually takes about ten years, according to Winick (1962).

A number of the older follow-up studies of addicts attempted to test the maturing out phenomenon (see Snow [1973] for a review of some of these studies). The results are ambiguous, partially due to problems with the data base. O'Donnell (1969), in his study of Kentucky addicts, found twelve subjects who had once been on the Bureau's list and were subsequently removed as inactive cases. Of these twelve, O'Donnell found that five had died, one was in prison throughout the five year period, three were continuously using narcotics, two spent part of their time in prison and subsequently became alcoholics (probably because they could not obtain narcotics), and only one man was completely abstinent for most of the five year period. If the same data inaccuracies, uncovered by O'Donnell, were found for addicts from other states, Winick's hypothesis would be seriously questioned.

In a further attempt to test the hypothesis, Ball and Snarr (1969) studied 242 addicts in Puerto Rico some thirteen years after onset of their opiate use. Two-thirds of their subjects either were still using heroin or were incarcerated. However, about a third had given up heroin use, and most of these were steadily employed and arrest-free. The authors conclude:

It appears then, that two major patterns exist with respect to the life course of opiate addiction in the United States. In one instance, the addict becomes increasingly enmeshed in a non-productive or criminal career as his dependence upon opiates progresses into his adult years. In the second case, the addict terminates his drug-centered way of life and assumes, or re-establishes, a legitimate role in society. In this latter sense, it may be said that some one-third of opiate addicts mature out of their dependence upon drugs. (Ball and Snarr, 1969: 10)

Another test of the maturation hypothesis was conducted by Mary Snow (1973). She divided a sample of 3,321 addicts reported to the New York City Narcotics Register into active and inactive cases, depending upon whether they had been again reported to the Register within a four-year period. She found that 23 percent were not re-reported, and she labelled these persons as "matured out." Seventy-four percent of these inactive cases as compared with 65 percent of the active cases were twenty-eight years of age or older. Thus, some support for Winick's hypothesis was offered.

In a more recent test of the maturation hypothesis, Maddux and Desmond (1981) defined abstinence as a period of no opioid use for three years. They found no high rate of onset of prolonged abstinence for any particular age group but did point to increasing abstinence with advancing age.

What do all these data mean? They probably mean that there is no firm support for the hypothesis, if by maturation one means that persons either give up the life after a period of ten years or until they enter their thirties. However, the data do indicate that as addicts become older they are more likely to give up the life.

The dynamics of this process were addressed by Leon Brill and his associates (1972). They studied 31 addicts who had been off narcotics for at least one year and for a median of three years. Brill, Nash, and Langrod (1972) hypothesized a "push-pull" theory of de-addiction. They reasoned that addicts were being pushed out of the life by the dire circumstances in which they found themselves. "Life becomes a rat race as the addict engages in the day-in, day-out 24 hour struggle to maintain his habit. Heroin use becomes extremely dysfunctional for most addicts and it is perceived as such by them" (Brill, 1972: 297). Addicts had increasingly larger habits to feed, were constantly placing themselves in jeopardy of arrest, were becoming tired of the life, and in some cases were suffering actual physical deprivation. Counterpoised to these pushes were the pulls of the legitimate, "square" life. These included the establishment of personal relationships within treatment facilities, the re-emergence of non-street addict goals and aspirations, and the possibility of legitimate employment, often as an ex-addict paraprofessional in a treatment program.

Most recently, Biernacki (1986) has applied the symbolic interaction perspective in explaining how addicts become abstinent on their own (that is, outside of the context of treatment). Fundamentally the process is one of identity transformation. Whether because of a traumatic event such as "hitting rock bottom" (being jailed or robbed, for instance) or a gradual disaffection with the addict life, persons resolve to leave the drug life. They do this by resurrecting prior nonaddict identities, by giving priority to non-addict self-concepts that may have emerged while the person was addicted or by creating new nonaddict selves. At the same time they make a conscious effort to shut out the addict world and demonstrate genuine behavioral and attitudinal commitment to more conventional activities. Those who have not completely severed such conventional activities find the road to abstinence more easily traveled.

Clearly all of these data can be put into the framework proposed here. As I hypothesized in Chapter 3, the greater both the role strain and the role conflict felt by the addict, the greater the likelihood of relapse. These data show that, as the addict ages, the requirements of the life become more burdensome. The constant "hustling" and "copping" and "hassles of the life" undoubtedly become increasingly difficult to bear—the street addict lifestyle is a demanding one. The addict feels increasing strain and inability to play the game. At the same time, the demands of nonaddict roles are lessened. Possibly, as Brill (1972) has pointed out, non-addict significant others lower their expectations about the addict and are willing to accept a conventionally less successful yet nevertheless drug-free individual.

Those who Stay in the Life

While it would appear that large numbers of addicts leave the "life" as they grow older, there is nevertheless a residuum of junkies who continue to use narcotics. Several studies have been conducted of these older addicts (Pascarelli and Fisher, 1974; Capel and Stewart, 1971; Capel, et al., 1972). These studies conclude that the aging addict must make some adjustments to his or her lifestyle. One of these compromises is seen in the choice of drug—while previously heroin was the favored drug, now Dilaudid may take its place because it is purer and can be taken orally. Preble and Miller (1977) noted that many junkies fall into the wine, welfare, and methadone syndrome whereby they enroll in methadone clinics, receive welfare payments, and combine the use of methadone and wine. While older addicts still cop from local pushers, their purchases are smaller possibly because of the expense involved or because the addict needs less substance than when he or she was younger. Hustling style is also affected, resulting in less physically demanding hustles, such as panhandling, petty crimes, and minor con games. Chief sources of income are more likely to be jobs, welfare, pensions, social security, or other legitimate sources. Thus, while still attempting to play the street addict role, the older addicts nevertheless must make some compromise with the inevitable process of aging. In essence, they become more marginal players on the scene.

Female Addicts

Throughout this chapter I have discussed the career of the street addict. Because most street addicts are male, I have focused primarily on the processes which are most relevant to them. Many of the same processes, of course, apply to the female addict. However, there are some noteworthy differences between the two. These differences are revealed in the types of roles which females often assume on the street. File (1976) developed a typology of such female-centered roles. First, and most frequently (57 percent of all female addicts), there is the hustler who earns her income through shoplifting and prostitution. Next in frequency is the worker (18 percent of female addicts) who is employed at least part time in a legitimate occupation; most workers also hustle on the side. Next in frequency, accounting for about 15 percent of female addicts, is the dependent addict. She usually relies on a male both for drugs and living money. There is also the drug seller who accounts for 8 percent of all female addicts. Finally, there is the bag follower. This is a special but rare type of female addict. The bag follower is a woman who is attached to a dealer and thus is easily able to obtain her drugs. These women, according to File, are usually white and attractive.

As can be seen from the above typology, most of the addict roles are stereotypically female. A substantial minority of the women are dependent upon men in a traditional fashion; the man provides both a livelihood and drugs to the women. Of those women who do support themselves, most are involved in activities associated with women—note that the criminal activities they engage in are shoplifting and prostitution. That much of female addict activity is sex-typed is documented by other studies of female addicts as well (Eldred and Washington, 1975, 1976; File, 1976; Rosenbaum, 1981).

In fact, these studies show that sex typing occurs throughout the career of the female street addict, from initiation to leaving the life. For instance, several studies have shown that female addicts are much more likely to have been first initiated into narcotics use by males than males are to have initially been "turned on" by a female. In fact, many women first begin to use narcotics within a relationship with a man. Once initiated, women are more likely to become addicted quicker and to have larger habits (seventy-five dollars a day for women compared to thirty-two dollars a day for men). Rosenbaum feels women have larger habits because it may be easier for them to make money through their prostitution. She also feels they become addicted quicker because, through their male lovers or husbands, they move into a world already populated by addicts. Women are also much more likely to obtain drugs from some route other than directly "copping" them. This is usually because they have a male who "cops" for them. Again, emphasizing the theme that women are more dependent on men, it was found that women are less likely to use drugs alone and more likely to "needle share" (that is, share their hypodermic needle with others). Finally, women might have more difficulty in leaving the life; Rosenbaum found that women were more permanently labelled as addicts than men were.

Summary

In this chapter, I have focused on the process of becoming a street addict. I have also addressed the maintenance of the addict role and the potential decline of the identity. It is clear that the concept of career applies to junkies. They become totally involved in an all-consuming lifestyle which provides an almost complete blueprint for living. And they experience both the rewards (status in their subculture and respect from their peers and sense of identity) and the costs (the dangers of health and freedom posed by the circumstances of the life) of the life. I believe the analysis presented in this chapter helps to further support the theory proposed in the previous chapter: becoming and being an addict supports the idea that heroin addiction is as much a commitment to a lifestyle as it is a dependency on a drug. Such a commitment is epitomized by the street addict role. How that role came to evolve in American society is a fascinating tale, and one I will tell in a later chapter. But first, let us explore alternative and more traditional theories of heroin addiction — the individualistic explanations.

Chapter Five

Individualistic Explanations for Heroin Use

In this chapter I shall briefly review and critique individualistic explanations for why people use and often become addicted to heroin. These are the physiologically based theories and the psychological/ psychiatric theories. I shall expend much more effort on the latter category of theories, because I do not believe it is unfair to say that they dominate the field today. Their hegemony is felt not only in the theoretical arena but they are heavily influential in shaping the form of treatment for heroin addiction.

I must admit to the reader that I pen this chapter with a great deal of trepidation. I do so for a number of reasons. First, I am not trained as a biologist, psychopharmacologist, psychologist, or psychiatrist. So I can always be subject to the charge that I do not fully understand the literature. Sometimes in engaging in debate with friends who are firm believers in individualistic approaches (especially psychiatrically based ones), I am accused of over-simplifying or "vulgarizing" the explanations. I shall attempt to avoid such stereotyping of theoretical positions. Secondly, I will not conduct an exhaustive review of this literature. A rather extensive volume could be devoted solely to this topic. I do not believe such a review is necessary to critique the major outlines of the approach. Thirdly, I must admit to a bias in this area. As I pointed out in the preface, in my twenty years of research experience in this field, I believe that I have too often observed the somewhat facile application of psychiatric labels to individuals whose life-styles violated the sensibilities and personal values of the professionally trained labellers. Finally, it is somewhat discomforting to "take on" a major portion of a field. While the individualistic explanations are certainly the Goliath of the field, I am not at all certain that I am up to playing the role of David.

Physiologically Based Theories

A reasonably large number of researchers have searched for a biological or genetic explanation for narcotics use. While it appears to me that these biologically based "disease" explanations are more fully developed for alcoholism (Fingarette, 1988; Peele, 1985, 1988) than for addictions to other types of psychoactive drugs, there nevertheless are a variety of physiologically based theories. (For a review of some of them, see Lettieri, Sayers, and Pearson [1980].) Probably the most extensive discussion and critique of the physiologically based "disease models" are provided by Peele (1985, 1988), and I shall draw extensively from his work.

Generally, for our purposes here we can say that there are several different varieties of physiologically based theories, which are not necessarily mutually exclusive. One of these—the metabolic deficiency theory—posits that some narcotic addicts react biochemically to narcotics in ways that other more "normal individuals" do not. Dole and Nyswander (1980) believe that when certain individuals are exposed to rather consistent use of a narcotic, their nervous systems undergo metabolic changes such that they must continue to use narcotics. (This is in fact the theoretical rationale for continued provision of methadone in methadone maintenance programs.) The analogy is often made to diabetics who must take insulin in order to live; some addicts, because of metabolic changes in their bodies, must continue to take narcotics in order to function normally. Some believe that these changes come about only after exposure to narcotics while others believe that some persons may be born with a predisposition to use narcotics. In other words, some individuals may be born with systems which already are somehow different from the majority of the population.

Genetic explanations are often employed to describe how and why individuals become addicted to various substances. Again, these arguments have probably been best developed in explaining alcoholism where the concordance rates between twins and between parents and their offspring (often when the child has been adopted out of the biological family in which one or both parents are alcoholic) have been most extensively studied. (For a good and largely supportive review of this point, see Goodwin [1988].) As regards genetic explanations of narcotic addiction, Peele (1985) notes some researchers have posited a linkage between a deficiency in endorphins, the body's own "naturally produced opiates," and narcotic addiction. It is argued that some individuals have an inbred endorphin deficiency which leaves them unusually sensitive to pain and hence more susceptible to becoming narcotic addicts in order to cope with this pain.

There are a number of criticisms of these disease models, and, as I have said, Peele (1988) does an outstanding job of critiquing them. First, for at least some theories like the metabolic deficiency theory, no specific metabolic mechanism has been identified. What exactly does this metabolic deficiency consist of? Secondly, there is not very much empirical research which directly supports the explanations. Most of it is hypothetical. For instance, it has not been empirically demonstrated (as far as I know) that narcotic addicts have metabolic deficiencies or a shortage of endorphins. Thirdly, many disease models posit a progressive and possibly irreversible pattern for the disease. For instance, once one starts to use narcotics, it is almost inevitable that one will continue to use more and more drugs to the point of physical addiction. There is now much evidence to indicate that many persons can use heroin and other narcotics recreationally and never become physically addicted to the narcotics (Zinberg, 1984). Similarly, there are many persons who can and do give up the use of narcotics without medical or treatment intervention. (See, for instance, Robins [1973] and Biernacki [1986].) How can this be if in fact they have a metabolic deficiency, which presumably would be permanent and indicate a probable life-long need for narcotics? Fourthly, many persons become "addicted" to a myriad of substances as different as cocaine (a central nervous system stimulant) and heroin (a central nervous system depressant). How can a single metabolic or organically based theory explain habituation to two such pharmacologically different drugs? In short, Peele (1985) makes the argument, with which I strongly agree, that the genetic and biological models presented here are too simplistic and appear to be unsupported by the currently available data. Habitual or regular use of psychoactive substances is simply too complex a phenomenon (involving physiological, psychological, and, most specifically, social and cultural factors) to be explained by a gene or a deficiency in one's biological makeup.

The Psychiatric/Psychological View of the Addict

There is an enormous amount of literature which has been produced by psychiatrists and clinical and research psychologists which attempts to explain why individuals use and/or become addicted to heroin and other psychoactive substances. An excellent and fairly extensive review of these studies is provided in Platt (1986). The reader is also referred to relevant theories as cited in Lettieri, Sayers, and Pearson (1980). Suffice it to say that most of these theories posit that the individual's psyche is in some way flawed and the individual uses psychoactive drugs to cope with or amelio-rate the emotional or intrapsychic distress, depression, or low self-esteem he or she feels. Many of these theorists would probably not subscribe to physiologically based or genetic theories of addiction. Yet I believe that many of the psychoanalytic, psychiatric, and psychological theories constitute a psychological-level disease model. They posit that there is something very wrong with the addict's emotional state and his or her ability to deal with emo-tional problems. The individual is, in other words, "emotionally" ill and needs to be "treated."

The Psychoanalytic Approach

This view of the addict as "ill" emanates from a variety of psy-chological-level perspectives. Psychoanalysts, psychiatrists, and clinical psychologists have contributed to various viewpoints about the origins and cures of this illness.

Let's look at some of the chief themes found in the works of psychoanalysts. Psychoanalysts, or those who derive their theo-retical orientations from Freud or his followers, have attempted to explain addiction with a particular emphasis on early childhood experiences, especially the interaction with the mother. Such theories are often more appropriate for explaining addiction among males than females. According to Platt (1986) various theorists have cited the role of maternal neglect and lack of love, maternal dominance coupled with passive and ineffectual father figures, and severe disappointment in an early love object (most often the mother) as factors which lead to inadequate ego development and the use of drugs to cope with the resultant "pain". Rado (1933) argues that the addict is often an individual whose ego has not matured as he grows older. Thus the original narcissistic state remains as his ideal. Because of inadequate ego development, the individual becomes tense and depressed. Heroin has two pronounced effects: an almost immediate orgasmic euphoria (achieved through an autoerotic injection into the arm called "booting" or "jacking off" in the streets) and an equally immediate reduction in physical discomfort and psychic pain. Drugs are used to alleviate this stress. In addition, use of heroin helps to control any aggressive tendencies the addict may feel. Because of physiological tolerance, the user must take more and more of the drug to achieve reduction in stress and pain. If the addict withdraws from heroin, three outcomes are possible: "(a) the individual goes through a drug free period for the sole purpose of resurrecting the effectiveness of the drug; (b) the individual succumbs to masochism and commits suicide, or (c) he descends into psychosis" (Platt, 1986: 127--128 citing Rado, 1933). I suppose a more hopeful outcome would be that the individual seeks treatment and resolves his ego problems. While the traditional viewpoint is that psychotherapy is not particularly effective in treating heroin addiction, others argue that it can be helpful (Ashery, 1983).

"The Inadequate Personality"

While the psychotherapists have advanced various theories for heroin addiction, their impact has been relatively minor. The predominant picture of the heroin addict has been painted by clinical psychologists who often employ both clinical insight and various personality inventories and other paper-and-pencil tests to determine the individual's psychological status. Again, it would be impossible to review this huge body of literature, and the reader is referred to a number of relatively recent reviews (Platt, 1986; Lang, 1983). Clinical studies have variously characterized addicts as: psychotic, neurotic, anxious, sadomasochistic, depressed, psychopathic, suffering from low self-esteem, hedonistic, limited in their ability to plan for the future, and sensation-seeking. In almost all cases, it is presumed that these personality characteristics preceded the addiction and thus "cause" the drug-using behaviors. Most fundamentally, drugs are used to help persons cope with the problems of living. If persons are psychotic, neurotic, depressed, or suffering from other problems, they use drugs to alleviate this distress.

For many years, much psychological research seems to have "been directed toward identification of specific predisposing characteristics in heroin addicts or demonstration of what has been called the 'addictive personality'" (Platt, 1986: 158). This common trait or set of personality traits (mostly those listed above) leads to the use of narcotics and other drugs. (Originally used to explain compulsive use of drugs and/or alcohol, the concept of addictive personality has been expanded to include compulsive eating, sexual activity, gambling, and other appetitive behaviors.)

Within the last few years, however, more and more researchers appear to be abandoning this concept. (There is still in my mind much doubt about whether treatment personnel, especially those who subscribe to a variant of the disease model of addiction, have seriously questioned the usefulness of the 'addictive personality' concept. More will be said about this in the chapter on treatment.) Nevertheless, researchers, as distinguished from practitioners, are clearly beginning to wonder whether all, or even most, narcotics addicts share a common personality trait. This is because the literature appears to be contradictory, failing to find consistent traits with which to characterize most addicts. After a fairly extensive review of this literature, Platt concludes:

> The most reasonable conclusion to draw based on available data, particularly the evidence presented in the studies reviewed in this chapter, would seem to be that although

addicts generally exhibit pathologic traits, there is a low probability that a common pattern of personality traits is present in all addicts. Thus, any attempt to specify an addictive type or addictive personality in terms other than a general level of disturbance will probably prove unproductive. (Platt, 1986: 164)

Similarly, Lang, after a very comprehensive review of the literature on the addictive personality, concluded that "no single, unique personality entity is a necessary or sufficient condition for substance abuse" (Lang, 1983: 218).

Critique of the Individualistic Approach

As I noted earlier in this chapter, the individualistic explanations still hold sway both in the research world and even more prominently in the treatment world. Some thinkers are now beginning to generate more comprehensive theories which to some extent modify the emphasis on the individual, and these will be discussed shortly. However, before we do this, let's review some of the criticisms of the more traditional individualistic approaches. These include the following:[1]

1) First, there is the "values" problem alluded to throughout this book. None of the social sciences or "helping professions" have reached the scientific stage of development where they can be considered "value free." Definitions of what constitutes "deviance" or "illness" must be placed within a social and cultural context. It is not surprising that a behavior that is so out of the mainstream as narcotics addiction would be labelled by most laymen and practitioners as a form of personality disorder. It is inevitable, then, that values play a large part in determining which behaviors are "sick." Remember, however, that even so called "scientific' clinical diagnoses are subject to changes due to more fundamental changes in society's values. The most prominent example of such a change was the downgrading of "homosexuality" from a clinically defective behavior to an alternative lifestyle by the American Psychiatric Association.

Zinberg (1984) paints a similar picture of marihuana use in American society. As he notes, the first generation of illicit drug users is always regarded as deviant. The second generation of users tries it out of curiosity or interest in its effects. "When the second generation supports the arguments of the first generation and opposes the cultural stereotypes about marihuana use and users, it is more likely to be heard; there are more of them; they are more diverse in background; and their motives, which seem less personal and less antagonistic to the reigning culture, are more acceptable to society" (Zinberg, 1984: 189). In other words, because of a change in values, a clinically disvalued drug use behavior becomes more acceptable to the society.

2) In addition to the fact that clinicians may knowingly or unknowingly be biased in their diagnosis of an individual, is the related point that the diagnostic instruments such as the Minnesota Multiphasic Personality Inventory (MMPI), one of the most frequently used instruments in this research, may itself contain such biases. One way it may contain such bias is in the "loaded" cultural content of some of its items. Junkies are asked to respond to items such as whether they like school, have been in trouble with the law, or have difficulties with their relatives. Items affirmatively answered help to contribute to diagnoses such as "psychopathic deviate." I would maintain that such items measuring the cultural realities of the street addict lifestyle and labelling them as indicators of psychopathy as such is itself culturally biased. (I would like to see a study conducted where the importance of individual items in the MMPI's subscales in determining diagnosis is determined. Such a study was conducted long ago in showing the cultural bias of the test for delinquents.)

Similarly, there is the problem of the groups which establish the "norms" of the tests. The MMPI and other personality inventories often determine the "illness" of individuals by the distance of their scores from a supposedly normal group. Such groups appear to be representative of the values and behavior of mainstream society. Yet heroin users are drawn from the world of the lower class, especially minority America—which may not fully share the values of the middle class in this country. In a fascinating series of studies, Gendreau and Gendreau (1970, 1971, 1973) show that there are no significant personality differences between narcotics addicts and nonusing controls when they are matched on socioeconomic status, opportunity to use narcotics, criminal history, age, and intelligence. In other words, when addicts are compared with persons who come from a similar milieu, differences between addicts and nonaddicts are minimal or nonexistent. Such findings suggest that the diagnostic and personality tests are more sensitive to cultural than individual differences between "mainstream controls" and addicts.

3) Very few of the studies of drug abusers (particularly heroin addicts) are longitudinal. Rather most studies are cross-sectional. Thus, relationships which are established between independent variables (personality types) and dependent variables (drug use) are only correlational. The types of longitudinal data necessary to establish causation (namely that one variable temporally precedes the other and is not spuriously related to it) are often not available to the researcher. For example, if one finds that addicts are depressed, one does not know whether the depression caused the addiction, whether it simply covaries with it, or whether it is a consequence of the addiction.

4) Related to this point is the fact that the samples of addicts on which most studies are based are usually institutionalized or captured samples. This fact has a number of ramifications. First, of course, is the question of how representative such samples are of the larger population of addicts from which they are nonrandomly drawn. (This criticism is applicable to virtually all studies of narcotics users because of the impossibility of choosing truly random samples of such users.) Remember that the concept of the inevitability of addiction following from the regular use of narcotics—so effectively challenged by Zinberg (1984)—emerged from studies of institutionalized patients. It was only when recreational users (whose controlled use of heroin obviated the necessity for treatment) were studied that the realization emerged that use did not necessarily lead to addiction. Secondly, there is always the issue of whether institutionalized addicts are even good representations of their ordinary, everyday selves. We know that addicts usually come into treatment when their behavior has become dysfunctional (Stephens and Ellis, 1975; Ellis and Stephens, 1976).

Thus, personality assessments taken at the time they are incarcerated (either in treatment or the criminal justice system) may not be reflective of their "true" personality. Thirdly, the personality instruments administered to addicts (often at the time of admission when they are most distressed) may measure transitory personality states. The fact that institutionalized addicts seem to score abnormally high on depression scales may be more a reflection of their psychological state attendant to their loss of freedom than as a more enduring personality trait.

Some More Recent Social Psychological Theories

Despite my rather strident criticism of the physiologically and psychologically based theories of drug use, there are a number of psychologically trained individuals who have contributed mightily towards a more complete understanding of this phenomenon. By and large, these individuals take a social-psychological approach and show how the phenomenon of drug taking (and other delinquent and deviant behavior) can be placed within a larger nexus of both personality and social variables. Most of these theories have focused on the development of drug use among adolescents and, hence, to a certain extent are limited to the beginnings of involvement in serious drug use. Also it should be noted that the largely middle-class adolescent research subjects in these studies did not demonstrate the heavy involvement with drugs as seen in the typical street addict pattern. Nevertheless, many of the insights gained from these studies are relevant to my own theory, and I should now like to review some of these theories and their relevance to my own perspective.

The Work of the Jessors

Probably one of the more comprehensive social-psychological attempts to explain drug use (largely marihuana use) and other problem behaviors is the work of Richard and Shirley Jessor. In a very complicated model they posit that two major clusters of antecedent/background variables influence social psychological variables. These two major antecedent clusters are "demography-social structure" (such as father's occupation, education, etc.) and "socialization" (parental ideology, home climate, peer, and media influence). The social psychological variables are composed of two clusters: the personality system and the perceived environment system. The personality system is composed of a number of variables which include the motivational-instigation structure (values about achievement, independence, affection, etc.), personal belief structure (alienation, self-esteem, etc.) and personal control structure (tolerance of deviance, religiosity, etc.). The perceived environment system is composed of a distal structure (parental and friends support and influence) and a proximal structure (parental and friends' approval of deviant behavior). These social-psychological variables, in turn, impact on problem behavior which is composed of drinking, marihuana use, premarital sex, and a number of other deviant behaviors. The path model proposed states basically that the antecedent-background variables determine the field in which the social-psychological variables then have their impact on creating and shaping problem behavior.

Much of the Jessors' work focuses on the role that the social-psychological variables play in the development of problem behavior. They believe that the personality structure strongly influences whether one engages in problem behavior. As the Jessors see it, the adolescent less likely to engage in problem behavior is one

> who values academic achievement and expects to do well academically, who is not concerned much with independence, who treats society as unproblematic rather than as deserving of criticism and reshaping, who maintains a religious involvement and is more uncompromising about transgression, and who finds little that is positive in problem behavior relative to the negative consequences of engaging in it. The adolescent who is more likely to engage in problem behavior shows an opposite personality

pattern—a concern with personal autonomy, a relative lack of interest in the goals of conventional institutions (such as school and church), a jaundiced view of the larger society, and a more tolerant attitude about transgression. (Jessor and Jessor, 1977: 237)

As regards the perceived environment, the Jessors find that it generally has somewhat greater explanatory ability than does the personality system. Particularly powerful are the proximal variables. They conclude:

The likelihood of occurrence of problem behavior should be greater the less the perception of parental support, the less the friends' control, the less compatibility in parent-friend expectations, and the greater the influence of friends relative to that of parents. Further, the less that parental disapproval is perceived and the greater the perception of friends approval and friends models, the more likely is problem behavior. These various measures point to the importance of whether the reference orientation is toward parents or toward peers. (Jessor and Jessor, 1977: 125)

In short, what Jessor and Jessor are saying is that the youth who engages in problem behavior seems to have a personal ideology and set of values which is supportive of deviant behavior. This world view is supported by friends who exist in the immediate environment and thus may have the most influence on the youth.

The Work of Elliott, Huizinga, and Ageton

In an even more sociologically related work, Elliott, Huizinga, and Ageton (1985) proposed a social-psychological model which integrated three major theoretical traditions: the strain, control, and learning theories. The first of these is strain theory as developed by Robert Merton. Very briefly, it posits that some youths may engage in deviant behavior because the society does not give them access to the legitimate means (such as well-paying jobs) to achieve material success in American society. Control theory, on the other hand, believes that the impulse towards committing deviant acts is always there; it is only through societal control and bonding to nondeviant values and others that one is prevented from committing deviant acts. Finally, learning theory notes that one learns, through a system of rewards and punishments, to commit and receive rewards from the commission of deviant behaviors. After testing their original path-analytic model on a national probability sample designed to be representative of American adolescents, the researchers developed a revised theory. They see delinquency and drug use emerging from a number of factors. Strain, inadequate socialization to the mainstream norms of the society, and social disorganization (such as the poverty and disorder of the slums) leads to weak bonding to conventional norms, values, and groups. Weak conventional bonding, as well as prior self-reported delinquency (and a direct path from social disorganization), lead to strong bonding to delinquent peers. Clearly, the data show that the central variable in the model is bonding to delinquent peers as measured by the subject's amount of time spent with peers, the delinquent activity of those peers, and the subject's assessment of the wrongness of committing certain deviant acts. The authors conclude: "these findings provide good support for the claims that bonding to delinquent peers is the most proximate cause of delinquency and drug use and that the effects of strain and conventional bonding are indirect and mediated by the level of bonding to delinquent peers. (Elliott, Huizinga, and Ageton, 1985: 142).

The central importance of the peer group has been repeatedly demonstrated in study after study (Kandel, 1974). Perhaps Oetting and Beauvais (in Peele, 1988) summarize the evidence best when they conclude from their own work that "peer drug associations are more highly related to drug use than any other psychosocial variable and, further, that the relationships between other psychosocial characteristics and drug use can be essentially accounted for by their influences on peer drug associations (Oetting and Beauvais, 1988: 147).

Stanton Peele's Work

As the reader can probably guess by now, I am generally a great admirer of the work of social psychologist Stanton Peele. I believe he has become an important and iconoclastic thinker in the fields of drug and alcohol abuse. I have relied heavily upon his work and thoughts in this chapter.

Peele has continued to develop his own theory of addiction, which he says is most recognizable as "an extreme, dysfunctional attachment to an experience that is acutely harmful to a person, but that is an essential part of the person's ecology and that the person cannot relinquish" (Peele, 1985: 97). While addiction has pharmacological and physiological concomitants, it is "the result of a dynamic social-learning process in which the person finds an experience rewarding because it ameliorates urgently felt needs, while in the long run it damages the person's capacity to cope and ability to generate stable sources of environmental gratification" (Peele, 1985: 97). Ultimately, Peele believes, addiction has its source in individual and cultural constructions of experience.

Peele then lays out the myriad of these social, cultural, and individual experiences. He sees the susceptibility to addiction and the choice of the addictive object (drugs, alcohol, food, persons, etc.) emanating from a number of sources. First, there are the social and cultural forces including social class, peer and parental influence, and culture and ethnicity. Secondly, there are the situational factors, including stress, social support and intimacy, and opportunity for enterprise and positive rewards. Finally, there are the individual factors which include the choice of the addictive object, the lack of values toward moderation, self-restraint and health, antisocial attitudes, aggression, alienation, lack of achievement, fear of failure, intolerance, uncertainty, belief in magical solutions, low self-esteem, lack of self-efficacy, and external locus of control.

Peele believes that persons become involved in addictive experiences because they need to have a sense of power and control and create satisfactory self-esteem. They desire simplification of their lives, predictability, and an immediacy of experience.

While I, too, believe many of these factors contribute to addiction to a substance, I cannot agree with many aspects of his argument. The "theory," through its inclusion of an enormous number of variables, simply defies the scientific canon of parsimony. More importantly, I believe that Peele's explanation still focuses on the "negative" aspects of drug use. That is, he appears to dwell too much on the escapist qualities of the addictive experience. He paints a picture of an addict who uses the drug or experience to cope with problems of living. While, as I have said throughout this book, I concur that this picture can certainly be painted of some narcotics addicts, I do not believe it is the predominant portrait. Addicts use drugs, I believe, for much more positive, role-affirming reasons.

Nevertheless, Peele moves the field along by emphasizing the importance of the social and cultural context in which drugs are used. His broadside attack on the "disease model," is beneficial and focuses the theoretical spotlight outside of the medical context. Further, his emphasis on the "moral" aspects of drug use (Peele, 1988) is refreshing. He maintains that persons' values (and the values of the groups to which they belong) help to determine whether they will become addicted and the shape that their addiction will take. His actors are much more "rational" in their behaviors and much more in control of their own destinies.

The Role of the Social Psychological Theories

My own sociocultural theory has benefited greatly from this social-psychological literature. And I believe that much of this literature supports, either directly or indirectly, much of the sociocultural perspective. Social psychologists acknowledge the premier place that the peer group's norms and values occupy in understanding drug use. Such a perspective is, of course, the linchpin of the sociocultural approach. Further, social psychologists recognize the importance of the larger social and cultural context in helping to determine and shape drug use patterns. Again, this is the bedrock on which the sociocultural perspective is built. Finally, these theorists recognize that the whole phenomenon of drug abuse is much more complex than simple physiological or genetic explanations.

The Sociocultural View

Having reviewed and critiqued these individualistic theories, I can briefly reflect on issues surrounding the sociocultural view of the typical individual addict's "psyche."

1. First, I do not deny that at least *some* addicts may now suffer or have suffered prior to addiction from an emotional disease. (We, of course, always have the classical "chicken and egg problem" of determining whether heroin use is the result of such illness or somehow directly or indirectly creates the distress.) But I do not believe that *most* addicts suffer from such psychiatric illnesses. They seem to function reasonably well in their own worlds. As we have seen, they are very successful criminals (at least as measured by the size of their criminal incomes), and they appear to be able to fulfill the other requirements of a rather demanding and complex role.

2. Fundamentally, the sociocultural viewpoint portrays most addicts as "rational individuals." That is, individuals, in the whole context of their own personal needs, social structural positions and culture, rationally choose (as much as any of us rationally decide the course of our lives) to follow the life of a street addict. It would seem that one does not need to turn to a psychopathology model in order to understand that these individuals act to fulfill the requirements of a role which they highly value. And, as Biernacki (1986) has shown, in an equally rational way, addicts decide to become abstinent either when they no longer can lead this lifestyle or it becomes incompatible with other roles they possess or decide to develop.

3. While virtually all of the psychological/psychiatric theories view heroin use as a means of escape, the sociocultural perspective sees it as a measure of involvement. While most theories see the addict as using heroin to cope with anxiety, distress or depression, the sociocultural approach views the use of heroin as a means of forging an existential identity. By this I do not mean to imply that the addict consumes drugs to "know himself" in the same way that some psychedelic drug users in the bygone "hippie era" may have used LSD (Stephens, 1982). Rather, I believe that

heroin and some closely related street drugs are "totems" or "badges" of membership in a close-knit society. One way that addicts demonstrate to others and themselves their commitment to the "street addict way of life" and reaffirm their self identities is to use heroin. Thus, they use heroin for "positive" reasons to demonstrate that they belong to a subculture and subscribe to its norms and values. Viewed in this way, heroin addiction is "proactive" rather than reactive.

4. The sociocultural model does not deny the importance of the physiological and narcotizing effects of heroin. But it does not see these effects as central to understanding why persons become addicted to heroin. Rather such effects can help us to understand more fully why persons may continue to take the drug. On the one hand, as Lindesmith (1968) points out, addicts continue to take drugs in order to avoid the pangs of withdrawal. Junkies usually state this as "taking care of or feeding their habit" or using drugs to "feel normal." On the other hand, as McAuliffe and Gordon (1974) demonstrate, addicts also desire to "get high" even after their habit is satisfied. That one can experience a euphoric, even escapist, sensation from the drug is only an added benefit to its use. Indeed, there are some researchers, such as Andrew Weil (1972), who claim that the desire to "get high" or change one's state of consciousness is inherent in individuals.

However, if persons take drugs in order to escape the pains of living, to cope with intrapsychic stress or as a result of some more fundamental underlying disorder, it is difficult to understand why individuals are often able, of their own free will, to give up the use of heroin. If the addicts described by both Biernacki (1986) and Rosenbaum (1981) are at all typical of those on the street, then the process they describe of "leaving the life" seems very natural and rational. They decide either that the "life" no longer appeals to them or they assume other roles which are incompatible with the street addict role (such as the role of mother). So they begin to distance themselves from heroin use and the lifestyle which accompanies it.

5. Even if drugs did provide that quick emotional fix that allowed one to cope with one's problems, I would still doubt that the seeking of this function would effectively explain drug abuse.

The chief reason is that the pharmacological action of these drugs seems to be so short-lived. Most heroin addicts I have talked with characterize the high, including both the "rush" and the "nod" as not lasting much more than about thirty to forty minutes. Would not the anxiety return after such a brief period of respite? Is the high so powerfully rewarding in and of itself to drive persons to continue to seek out drugs for these very brief periods of relief from such emotional pain and agony?

6. I am certain that many readers might want to know how anyone could say that heroin users in some way or other are not emotionally abnormal. After all, who in their right mind would knowingly take substances that are potentially deadly and involve themselves in a life-style which is dangerous and, on the whole largely unattractive?[2] As I have repeatedly said throughout this volume, it is difficult to view this world from a middle-class perspective. As a middle class individual, the street addict life-style is not my "cup of tea." But that does not mean the life is unappealing to others. In fact, as many of the studies cited herein show, the lifestyle—from the viewpoint of those in it—is both rewarding and exciting. It is dangerous and often those who live in it are depressed about themselves. (Of course, most people experience depression and misgivings about at least some aspects of their lives.) Yet there also are many rewards, as well. Indeed, the intensity of the "peaks" and "valleys" of the typical addict career may actually make the life even more exciting and appealing.

My students often "intellectually buy" what I am saying but tell me in their heart of hearts, they really don't accept the argument. Again, the reluctance is based on the belief heroin is such a dangerous and addictive substance that sane people would never willingly use it. But consider the case of another highly addictive substance which has been shown to be highly toxic. It has been linked to many different types of cancer, to heart disease and to a whole host of other maladies. It costs the nation hundreds of millions of dollars in lost worker productivity and in health costs. Persons often have a lifelong addiction to this drug even though they know it is bad for them and though many have tried numerous times to "give it up." While its immediate physiological and mind-altering effects are not as pronounced as heroin's, its use nevertheless appears to be both highly rewarding and at the same time its denial appears to be very distressing to its users. I am, of course, speaking of tobacco.[3] (Similar analogies can be made about the overconsumption of food and alcohol, and maybe even sex.) Yet I am hard pressed to find the students who are willing to label such smokers as emotionally ill. Nor would they advocate the institutionalization of such individuals. The point is that when behavior, although probably objectively irrational, moves closer to that of middle-class life, it becomes more "normal" and more understandable.

7. There is finally the point that heroin use, especially frequent use, is concentrated heavily in the lower class and there occurs disproportionately among minority groups. There are three possible explanations for this finding. First, it may be that the underlying disease, of which heroin addiction is a symptom, occurs more frequently in lower-class and minority groups. The reasons for such a finding have variously been seen as genetically, socially, and/or culturally based (Peele, 1985). Secondly, it may be that while the basic underlying disease is spread more proportionately throughout the total population, these groups respond to stress by taking heroin while others may react in other ways (through alcoholism or other forms of deviant behavior). The sociocultural approach would posit a third explanation, namely. that the street addict role is one of a relatively limited number of roles in the areas in which it occurs. Further, many people—at least those in the subculture—value this role and adopt it for positive identity creating reasons.

We shall now turn our attention once more to the street addict role and in the next chapter explore how it came to be.

Chapter Six

Origins of the Street Addict Role

"Where did the street addict role come from?" As we shall see, the answer is not a simple one; a complex mix of historical, political, social, economic, cultural, and other forces combined to eventually lead to the development of this role in twentieth-century America.

Narcotic Addition in America Prior to the Twentieth Century

A historical perspective is particularly important here for it has not always been true that narcotic addicts were largely drawn from the ranks of the lower class and urban minorities. Indeed, in the latter part of the nineteenth century and possibly into the early part of this century, there is a good deal of evidence to indicate the predominant type of narcotic addict was a white, middle- to upper-class woman who often lived in the South. These women were iatrogenic addicts; that is, they were physically habituated to narcotics by their physicians. The tale of these women is an interesting one. They often lived in constricted social worlds. They were not allowed to be employed and had limited social contacts outside of the home. While many of them undoubtedly suffered from legitimate physical complaints, it is also believed that many endured psychosomatic illness brought on by frustration and boredom. They possessed economic resources which enabled them to obtain relief offered by the popular patent medicines of the day. Because narcotics (and indeed all psychoactive substances) were not illegal at that time, over-the-counter medications, like "Scotch Oats Essence" and "Mother Winslow's Soothing Syrup," often con-

125

tained opium or other narcotics. The narcotics, being central nervous system depressants, produced relief from both physical pain and anxiety.

When these women turned to physicians, they often were prescribed narcotics. During most of the nineteenth century, medical knowledge was still in a fairly rudimentary state. The "germ theory" was not accepted until the latter part of the century, and since physicians did not know the etiology of many diseases, they could not address the root causes of illness. Often the physician was able to treat only the symptoms of the disorder. Since pain is one of the primary symptoms of many illnesses, the physician frequently reached into his little black bag only to pull out a narcotic compound. He was often aided in providing more instant and complete surcease from pain through use of the newly invented hypodermic needle.

While these female iatrogenic addicts probably constituted the largest group of narcotic addicts in the country, they were by no means the only type of addict. Many veterans of the Civil War had become addicted to narcotics on the battlefield and came to rely on them for relief from pain caused by chronic conditions acquired during the war. In fact, morphinism was sometimes known as the "soldier's disease."

Probably more important for our discussion here was a type of addict found in the cities of America. These were the narcotics addicts who frequented the "opium dens." The practice of opium smoking was imported into this country by the Chinese who emigrated to the West Coast in search of their fortunes. Many of these Chinese men had hoped to use the money from their employment to allow them eventually to return to China, where they could lead comfortable lives. Instead, they became trapped here in America filling service jobs at the lowest level. Often employed as waiters, laundry workers, and railroad laborers, they led lonely, desperate lives. One of the few ways they could escape the rigors of their existence was to spend a few reverie-filled hours in the opium dens.

According to Courtwright (1982), this pattern quickly spread to white members of the underworld. Professional criminals, gamblers, prostitutes, and others in the "fast life" soon became attracted to the practice of smoking opium. Indeed, prostitutes sometimes utilized narcotics as a crude form of birth control, relying upon the physiological fact that narcotics can disrupt the menstrual cycle. Courtwright claims that a type of subculture developed in the opium den which was a "meeting place, a sanctuary, and a vagabond's inn" (Courtwright, 1982: 73). Denizens of these opium dens were not only taught the techniques of use but were also indoctrinated with a set of rules which specified no violence or theft from others on the premises. Prophetically, these dens became the precursor of the street addict subculture we observe today. As Courtwright says: "In virtually all particulars—peer reinforcement, exclusive membership, common argot, and shared rules of appropriate behavior—opium smoking anticipated the pattern of the various twentieth-century drug subcultures" (Courtwright, 1982: 74).

This, then, was the situation in the United States at the dawn of the twentieth century. Except for some state and local statutes, narcotics were, by and large, freely available. Virtually all pharmacies had various opium-containing preparations which could be sold over the counter. As previously noted, many patent medicines contained narcotics or other psychoactive substances. Indeed, there was even a new cocaine preparation marketed as "Coca-Cola."

Historical Forces for Change

About the turn of the century, the winds of public opinion began to change course. While the American populace and its political leaders heretofore had largely been tolerant of narcotics, a complex of new forces merged to create calls for reform. (The story is very complicated and parts of the tale are variously described in a number of excellent historical treatises by Lindesmith [1968], Duster [1970], Courtwright [1982], Musto [1973], Morgan [1981], and Helmer [1975].) Among those forces were: international and diplomatic concerns, domestic moral concerns, race and social class bias, and changes in the medical profession.

We will now very briefly review these pressures for change.[1] First, there were international and diplomatic concerns. It was clear that in many ways the twentieth century was to be dominated by the United States. The initial stirrings of this manifest destiny were felt at the beginning of this century. Because of both economic and political concerns, the U.S. took a leadership role in the world community concerning the problem of narcotics. No doubt this was partly due to reaction to the "enslavement" to narcotics of millions of peasants in China and to the resultant Opium War. As a part of this leadership role, the U.S. played a major part in antinarcotics international conferences in Shanghai and in The Hague. The net effect of these conferences was to call for international control of the narcotics trade—mirrored in American domestic legislation to curb and control narcotics use.

At the same time, many U.S. religious leaders and moral crusaders decried the problem of narcotic addiction at home. Possibly because of subtle demographic changes in the makeup of the American narcotic addict population and no doubt due to racist sentiment, the drug addict was seen as less benign. From the status of a sick individual, more and more Americans came to see narcotic addicts as criminally responsible for their own behavior. There was a strong current of moral outrage directed at all substance use, including alcohol (Gusfield, 1963), which was soon to be outlawed.

As both Gusfield (1963) and Helmer (1975) point out, this moral outrage was to some extent fueled by fear of blacks, Mexicans, and European immigrants drawn from populations other than those from which most Americans had previously come. These groups not only had strange customs, but many Americans believed they competed for jobs traditionally held by American citizens. Alcohol use was associated with largely Catholic immigrants, while use of other types of substances was identified with other disvalued ethnic groups. Opium use was the habit of the Chinese, who were willing to take on jobs at lower pay levels than anyone else. Marihuana use was associated with Mexicans who came across the border to compete with American farm laborers. And finally, the use of cocaine in soft drinks was associated with blacks in the south. It was especially feared that black males who used cocaine would become sexually stimulated and would yield to their supposed uncontrollable desire for white women.

Finally, there were both economic and scientific changes in the medical profession. As I noted earlier, medicine and pharmacology began to be based more in science than in folk remedy. As physicians came to be able to treat the root causes of disease and illness, the narcotic panacea declined in relative importance. Both physicians and pharmacists yearned for higher social status and the financial rewards which often accompany elevation in social position. Then, too, they were embarrassed by the public knowledge that they were directly responsible for much of the narcotic addiction in America. They felt a need to change this image and exercise more direct control over the dispensing of narcotics and similar substances in the future.

Passage of the Harrison Act

All of these forces began to merge and provide the impetus for solution. After a fair amount of debate, the United States Congress in 1914 passed a relatively mild law known as the Harrison Act. The law rather innocuously called for the licensing and taxation of those who produced and dispensed narcotics. Most importantly, the law provided that individuals could use narcotics only with a physician's prescription and then only for a legitimate medical use.

That phrase "only for a legitimate medical use" has had profound ramifications for the United States. Many (including myself) who have studied the issue in much more detail, believe that this marked the turning point for psychoactive substances in American life. By power of the Harrison Act, a series of Federal bureaucracies, composed of persons trained in law enforcement, had been given the task not only of enforcing the anti-drug laws but in interpreting them, as well.

A very strict and harsh interpretation of the Harrison Act was made almost before the ink was dry on the document. Federal agents, eventually to be led by famed "moral entrepeneur" Harry Anslinger, read the law to mean that addicts could not be maintained on narcotics because maintenance was not within the meaning of "legitimate medical purpose." Federal agents saw to it that both individual physicians and the narcotics maintenance clinics of the

twenties were prohibited from dispensing narcotics for maintenance purposes. Persons who were previously addicted had two
choices: give up their narcotics use or become criminals.

No doubt many addicted southern women and other more mainstream individuals chose the former course (O'Donnell, 1969).
However, it is apparent that many chose the latter course, as well.
I would suspect that many such individuals already were seen as
criminals because, in fact, that is how they earned their money. As
I have stated elsewhere, I believe that the Harrison Act and the
increasingly punitive federal and state legislation which followed
had other profound ramifications. Because heroin and other narcotics were now illegal, the price of the commodity rose drastic-
ally. The increasingly harsh penalties associated with sale of the
drug only drove the cost higher. The drug was "cut" more and
more so that much more "drug" could be sold per kilogram of
pure heroin. Heroin itself became a more popular drug because a
"bigger bang for the buck" could be obtained with a smaller, and
thus more easily transported and concealable, quantity. Addicts
began more and more to favor the use of the hypodermic needle
over other routes such as smoking and "snorting." Again, this was
no doubt due to the economic changes wrought by the law. Intravenous injection provides the most efficient way of getting the best
high with the smallest quantity of drug.

In my view, probably the most profound effect of the anti-drug
laws was to create a clandestine drug distribution and sales network
which was fueled by enormous profits. (Today a kilogram of raw
opium, worth only several thousand dollars on the black market
where it is grown, is worth over a million dollars on the streets of
an American city.) In addition, the laws helped to create a tightly
knit network of users and sellers. Salespersons at the street level of
the distribution network were almost always themselves addicts.
Users needed to band together to protect themselves from law
enforcement officials. In a highly secretive environment, they were
able to share information about who had the best drugs. They also
were able to learn the techniques of how to use drugs. Finally, they
were compelled, given the high cost of drugs, to turn to income-
generating criminal activities in order to support their habits.

Sometime after World War II, another rather profound change seemed to occur. Heroin use moved heavily into lower-class areas of large cities, particularly the barrios and ghettos of the nation. Claude Brown chronicles the emerging role that heroin played in Harlem at about this time:

But something else happened that summer—something that made things change...Horse was a new thing, not only in our neighborhood but in Brooklyn, the Bronx and every-place I went, uptown and downtown. Everybody was talk-ing about it. All the hip people were using it and snorting it and getting this new high. To know what was going on and to be in on things, you had to do that. And the only way I felt I could come out of Wiltwik (a facility for juvenile delinquents) and be up to date, the only way to take up where I had left off and be the same hip guy I was before I went to Wiltwyck, was to get in on the hippest thing and the hippest thing was horse." (Brown, 1965: 99-100)

The reasons for this movement into the lower-class areas of cities has not been well documented in the professional literature. I can speculate on some of the causes. First, it is apparent that nar-cotic addiction can flourish only in a relatively secretive environ-ment. That is, heavy law enforcement presence in all likelihood precludes the development and growth of drug sales and consump-tion networks. It is probably true that police have historically been less interested in and more tolerant of drug related activities in lower class neighborhoods than in areas where the citizenry are more politically powerful.

Secondly, as I pointed out earlier in the discussion of the opium dens, there was always narcotics use in the criminal subculture. It is most likely true that for much of the twentieth century many criminals, prostitutes, gamblers, and other habitues of the under-world have used drugs at least some of the time. To the extent that these criminal types lived in or frequented lower-class areas of the community, the distribution and use of narcotics may already have gained an early foothold in these areas. Certainly these areas provided vast new profit potential for organized crime which was at the top of the importation and distribution networks.

Thirdly, it is also true that members of the "life" frequented these areas. Besides professional criminals, prostitutes and gamblers who were all part of the "life", many other persons lived in the "fast lane." Particularly noteworthy are many jazz figures who at the time were both heroin users and major ghetto folk heroes. Bessie Smith and "Bird" Parker are just two examples. These individuals, to some extent, may have been role models to at least some residents of the ghetto.[2]

Fourthly, I believe that heroin use and the attendant street addict role may have fallen on fertile subcultural soil. It may have been supported by at least some aspects of lower-class lifestyles, and it is to this point that I will now devote some extensive attention.

Lower-Class Lifestyles

A number of researchers (Lewis, 1966; Miller, 1958; Gans, 1962; Rainwater, 1970; Hannerz, 1969; Liebow, 1967; Stack, 1974; Anderson, 1978; MacLeod, 1987) have studied the conditions of lower-class and ghetto life in America. Some of them have argued that the lower-class way of life is different enough from mainstream American life as to constitute its own subculture. We shall briefly review this work to see if it can inform us further about the origins of the street addict world. (An excellent, if somewhat dated, review and critique of some of the earlier work is available in Valentine [1968].)

The general picture of the lower class painted by these authors is one of separateness and alienation from the larger society. Lower-class values, beliefs, and behaviors are described as distinct from those of the larger American society. The lower class is characterized as politically apathetic with little concern for participation in the larger culture. There is little community structure beyond the immediate family unit. Families are often headed by women. The males, who have little role in the socialization of the children, live in a world with scant economic or social stability. The relationships between the sexes are often fleeting and are sometimes said to constitute serial monogamy. Children are socialized early on by the peer group and through this socialization and lack of other opportunities, the children in turn adopt this subculture. In turn, through the natural cycle of life, they pass it on to their children.

Walter Miller (1958) argues that the lower-class way of life is governed by a number of focal concerns. One of these is a preoccupation with "trouble" which includes law breaking, sexual adventurism, and fighting. Sometimes trouble confers prestige (as in a delinquent gang) or sometimes it is "implicitly recognized as a means to other valued ends, e.g., the covertly valued desire to be 'cared for' and subject to external constraint, or the overtly valued state of excitement or risk. Very frequently 'getting into trouble' is multi-functional, and achieves several sets of valued ends" (Miller, 1958: 8.) Another focal concern is "toughness" which includes masculinity and physical prowess. There is also "smartness" which involves "the capacity to outsmart, outfox, outwit, dupe, 'take', 'con' another" (Miller, 1958: 9.) Yet another focal concern is "excitement," or the constant search for thrills and flirting with danger. "Fate" is also of central concern to the lower-class. It is represented by the feeling that fortune or luck is extremely important in determining the course of one's life. There is also the concern for "autonomy," which finds expression in the desire for freedom from control by others. Miller maintains that lower-class males will overtly express the desire for complete autonomy— illustrated by the sentiment that "no one's gonna push me around." Yet covertly, lower-class persons will often foster dependency, as in the case of delinquent boys who run from correctional institutions in an attempt to activate efforts to return them.

These various focal concerns interact with one another in such a way as to create a distinctive lower-class way of viewing and acting towards the world. Miller (1958) stresses that the lower class person (particularly the delinquent youth who is the focus of his essay) acts to achieve status through behavior which conforms to the community's values. As he says, "No cultural pattern as well-established as the practice of illegal acts by members of lower class corner groups could persist if buttressed primarily by negative, hostile, or rejective motives; its principal motivational support, as in the case of any persisting cultural tradition, derives from a positive effort to achieve what is valued within that tradition, and to conform to its explicit and implicit norms" (Miller, 1958: 19).

The assertions of the uniqueness and permanence of lower class value systems by Miller (1958), Lewis (1966), and others have generated much criticism. Partly, this is due to assertions by Parsons (1951) and Merton (1957) that Americans, including the lower class, share a single system of values.

Others, such as Valentine (1968), argue that subcultural theorists have ignored or glossed over several important aspects of the subculture concept. Valentine believes that the lower class shares many of the same values as do middle- and upper-class individuals. In fact, many of the so-called focal concerns, such as toughness or smartness, are also found in the middle class; they may simply express themselves in different ways. Further, Valentine argues that the emphasis on the perpetuating lower-class subculture smacks of "blaming the victim." The structural and economic conditions under which members of the lower-class live account for as much of their behavior and values as does their so-called subculture. The concern with immediate gratification, the instability of the traditional family unit, and the belief in fate may all be by-products of the job instability and economic precariousness of lower-class and ghetto life. If these conditions change, the argument goes, much of the "uniqueness" of lower-class subcultural values disappear. Finally, much more ethnographic and empirical research needs to be done to resolve the debate.

Rodman (1963) offers a compromise between these two positions. He maintains that the lower class utilizes a "value stretch" in order to adjust to deprived circumstances. Without abandoning the general values of the society, members of the lower class "stretch" the values of the larger society. Such stretching is needed to create an alternative set of values which is more consonant with the structural and economic realities of lower-class life. Rodman conceives of these alternative values as lower-class cultural resources which "come to compensate for [the] lack of social and economic resources" (Rodman, 1963: 214).

In an insightful discussion of black lower class values and the identity structures which result, Rainwater (1970)—who studied the black Pruitt-Igoe housing development in St. Louis—makes several telling points. First, he agrees with Rodman's position that lower-class persons are compelled to adapt to the realities of the structural position in which they find themselves. For blacks, the two main structural realities are their economic marginality and the society's racial oppression. Poor people live among others who are equally marginal in economic terms and, because of this situation, place a premium on the exploitation and manipulation of peers. As he says: "The individual's daily experience teaches him that his peers are dangerous, difficult and out to exploit him or hurt him in petty or significant ways" (Rainwater, 1970: 371). Further, in lower class life there is an emphasis on "stripped down" ways of organizing social roles and relationships. Persons interact with others in simpler and less elaborate ways, and there is less stability and permanence in their interaction.

Because of these structural and interactional constraints, it is more difficult for a lower-class person to establish what Rainwater calls a "valid identity"—a sense of self-esteem and worth which is reinforced by others. Rainwater says: "If a valid identity does not lie in the direction of a viable economic role (either directly or in the purely instrumental terms of allowing a man to be a good provider or a woman to be a good housekeeper and mother), then one must seek in other ways to construct a self which provides some measure of gratification of needs and earns some measure of recognition of oneself as a social being" (Rainwater, 1970: 377).

Such valid identity is found in what Rainwater calls an "expressive lifestyle." The "expressive lifestyle" consists of highly stylized and often deviant activity which finds middle-class acceptance only in the realms of entertainment or sports. Involvement with alcohol, drugs, gang fighting, and sexual activities are all manifestations of this "expressive lifestyle." "The culture encourages individuals to seek idiosyncratic and nonrational experiences, such as fighting as a self-maximizing mode of relating to the world... or sexual activity as a way of presenting the self as unique and power-ful. In all of these activities two things are going on at the same time: the individual is experiencing a heightened sense of himself as a total being and he is accumulating an attractive social identity" (Rainwater, 1970: 379).

In studying one Washington, D.C., ghetto neighborhood, Hannerz (1969) discovered that ghetto life was more complex than at least some other researchers had portrayed it. He found at least four different lifestyles in the ghetto. The first of these is the "mainstreamers," or those persons who most closely conform to conventional American values and norms. These people attempt to hold jobs, to own and keep their homes in good repair, and, in general, to have more middle-class family-oriented values. Next, are the "swingers," who are usually single and young. Among the "swingers" the emphasis is on partying and sociability. They seek variety and entertainment and often are only sporadically employed. The third group, the "street families," are more like the stereotypical female centered loosely knit black families portrayed by Stack (1974). Finally, there are the street-corner men who are likely to be found "hanging out" at all hours of the day and night on the street corners. These men are often unemployed and some-times turn to crime (especially street crime) to supplement their meager incomes. The world of the streetcorner men centers on use of alcohol (and other drugs) and is often punctuated by violence.[3] Thus there is no single set of norms and values to which all ghetto dwellers subscribe. Rather there is an unclear demarcation among the values and norms of all these groups (who are to some extent tied together by the concept of "soul") and between the values of these groups and mainstream American society.

Nevertheless, Hannerz detects themes which he calls a "ghetto-specific complex":

Among the components of this ghetto-specific complex are for instance female household dominance; a ghetto-specific male role of somewhat varying expression including, among other emphases, toughness, sexual activity, and a fair amount of liquor consumption; a relatively conflict-ridden relationship between the sexes; rather intensive participation in informal social life outside the domestic domain; flexible household composition; fear of trouble in the environment; a certain amount of suspiciousness toward other persons' motives; relative closeness to religion; particular food habits; a great interest in the music of the group; and a relatively hostile view of much of white America and its representatives. (Hannerz, 1969: 177)

In short, these features describe a ghetto subculture.[4]

Emergent Themes From This Literature

Whether one believes there is a general ghetto lifestyle or subculture or that it is composed of a number of different lifestyles, I believe there are certain themes which wind throughout all of the work cited above and help us to understand both the source of the street addict role and its place in the world of lower-class America.

The first, and most important, theme is that the role is found in a world characterized by limited economic opportunities. Because many persons, particularly the young, are under-educated, they possess few job market skills which are saleable outside the slum. Often, too, because of racism and other structurally imposed constraints, they are barred from meaningful economic and social participation in the world outside the ghetto. Thus the street addict role (or other peripheral street corner and often illegal roles) is one of the few options available to the person. The second theme is that persons often turn to these roles because they want to react to the sense of "failure" they often feel. While it is true that there is a ghetto subculture, it is also true that mainstream culture, especially in its definitions of material success and the role of the male breadwinner, is heavily felt in lower-class society. The inability of the male to play this role leads to a profound sense of failure. A number of researchers have pointed to the importance of this sense of failure as a reason for persons to seek out lifestyles other than the dominant culture prescription for male behavior. As Liebow says: "The streetcorner is, among other things, a sanctuary for those who can no longer endure the experience or prospect of failure. There, on the streetcorner, public fictions support a system of society at large, make for a world of ambivalence, contradiction, and paradox, where failures are rationalized into phantom successes and weaknesses magically transformed into strengths" (Liebow, 1967: 214).

Accordingly, persons develop alternative roles which can be played in the ghetto or lower-class setting and which give rewards to the actors. Hannerz (1969) describes the ghetto-specific male role alternative which is particularly found among "male swingers and streetcorner men. It is centered about these concerns: (1) strong overt concern with sexual exploits; (2) emphasis on toughness and ability to command respect from others; (3) preoccupation with personal appearances, with a particular emphasis on male clothing fashions; (4) high liquor (and sometimes drug) consumption; (5) high verbal skills and competence in speaking in the ghetto slang; and (6) admiration for the trickster or "con man".

A third theme drawn from this literature is that the identities of many ghetto dwellers depends largely on the influence of the peer group. Much emphasis is put on sociability and "hanging out" in the lower-class environment. This seems particularly true for the street-corner men, both adolescents and adults. Recent research (MacLeod, 1987) documents the enormous amounts of time spent with the peer group by both lower-class white and black males. Similarly, Anderson's (1978) analysis of the clique of men who "hang out" in a local liquor store clearly indicates that much investment in both time and emotion is made by these men. It is not surprising then that the peer group assumes enormous importance in providing a valid identity to these men.

It is apparent, then, that the street addict role has developed out of and is supported by some parts of the lower-class ethos; there are many elements of overlap. In looking at Miller's and Rainwater's work, we can see that there is a general set of world views which is not dissimilar to that of the street addict role portrayed in Chapter 3. Virtually all of the focal concerns described by Miller (1958) are characteristics of the street addict role. The street addict is desirous of being seen as tough, smart, autonomous, and adventurous. Similarly, the distrust of other persons and the concern with being manipulated, highlighted by many of the researchers reviewed here, is a hallmark of the street addict identity. The overlap between the ghetto specific male role described by Hannerz (1969) and the street addict role is noteworthy. And, of course, the street addict role is the very epitome of the expressive lifestyle as outlined by Rainwater (1970).

Again, I want to reemphasize that I am not saying that all lower-class persons or ghetto dwellers share the same norms and values. It is clear from the literature reviewed in this chapter that they do not. However, there are certain themes, particularly found among delinquent gangs, streetcorner men and "swingers" and to a lesser extent among others in these settings, which are supportive of many of the street addict values and norms.

In summary, the origins of the street addict role are both structural and cultural. Most addicts are products of environments where there are severely limited opportunities for "success," at least as defined by the larger society. This is a direct result of both the social-structural conditions of American society and the social class and ethnic prejudice which still exists.

But it is also due to certain cultural conditions as well. Street addicts, most of whom emanate from lower class and ghetto settings, seem to have borrowed heavily from the values and norms of the larger subculture in which they grew up. They have changed these general norms and values when necessary, in order to adapt them to the exigencies of being a street addict.

As we have seen, the nature of narcotics addiction in America dramatically changed in the relatively short period of a century. Prior to the Harrison Act, narcotics use (especially recreational and euphoria-seeking use) was, by and large, unknown to lower class Americans, except for some of those in the criminal underworld. One possible effect of the Harrison Act and subsequent piece of anti-drug legislation was to focus it in locales less subject to legal control. These locales were the ghettoes and slums of America where law enforcement, either because of neglect or the inability to enforce the laws, was most lax. It was here also where some cultural values supportive of narcotics use were found and where social-structural conditions limited access to many meaningful roles. Because of these social structural conditions and attendant subcultural support, heroin use moved out of a limited world of opium dens and use among professional criminals to the larger slum setting. This street addict expressive lifestyle which gave dignity and a sense of belonging and success to many alienated and disenfranchised individuals.

Postscript: Structural Symbolic Interactionism

As I noted in Chapter 2, one criticism of symbolic interactionist theory is that it is astructural; some claim it ignores the very real variable of social structure. In this chapter, I have tried to lay that criticism to rest. For I believe I have shown that the street addict role was created and shaped by both social-structural and cultural factors.

Chapter Seven

Treatment for the Street Addict

As the reader probably can guess by now, I am often critical of many treatment efforts currently employed to help the street addict; this flows from my critique of the individualistic approaches outlined earlier. (For an even more damning indictment, see Peele [1985].)

It is upon these psychological/psychiatric approaches that treatment is primarily grounded, both theoretically and pragmatically. My skepticism, however, is not so complete that I feel treatment should be abandoned. To the contrary, I believe that treatment can and often does have a very meaningful place in helping to solve the "drug problem" in America. In this chapter, I hope to "flesh out" this theme by reviewing each treatment modality, its strengths and weaknesses. Further, I hope to show how the socio-cultural approach developed in this book might help us to understand the potential efficacy of treatment as well as aid us to shape current and new treatment modalities.

The Hegemony of the "Sickness Model"

Before we review each of the treatment modalities individually, however, we must examine the general principle of treatment as it applies to the street addict. The very word "treatment" implies that there is an "illness" which needs to be treated. The standard medical model applies. You first recognize that you are ill, usually by the presence of uncomfortable symptoms. Then you go to the doctor who treats you with some medication or other prescribed regimen to make you well. Likewise the addict has an illness which is diagnosed by its symptoms. The most readily recognizable symptom is the substance abuse itself. Addiction to a chemical is indicative of a deeper underlying condition. This condition rests in the emotional makeup of the individual—in his or her psyche. Once this underlying etiological condition is successfully treated, the person's need for narcotics or other psychoactive substances will be eliminated, and that person can then go on to lead a healthy and drug free life.

It seems to me that whatever their own individual orientations, virtually all treatment modalities in this country accept, in one form or another, the characterization of the "sick" individual portrayed above. Most treatment providers probably embrace the notion of the addictive personality, which I described and critiqued earlier. As I have also said, I, and an increasing number of research professionals in the field, have great difficulty in accepting this portrayal of the average street addict. Rather I see the addict largely as a "rational" or emotionally "normal" individual who chooses to live the street addict life for a variety of complex reasons outlined in the previous chapters.

If my perspective—that most street addicts are probably emotionally "normal" individuals—is correct, then what role does treatment play? I believe that treatment can play a very important role in helping addicts to leave the life if they so desire. That treatment intervention is not a necessary condition for leaving the life is well documented by Biernacki (1986). For many individuals, however, treatment intervention can provide needed assistance in helping the person to "get his or her act together."

Commonalities in Treatment Programs

Each modality contributes in its own unique way to this endeavor. However, there are also some commonalities in the way that treatment, in whatever form, generally helps the individual to abandon the life of the street addict. First, of course, almost all treatment modalities provide some sort of respite from that powerful imperative of the addictive street lifestyle—the need to continually "cop" and use heroin. Many programs provide some sort of detoxification or substitute drug so that addicts, in their quest to avoid withdrawal, no longer are consumed by the need to seek out drugs every eight hours or so. Thus the chemical impetus to remaining in the drug life is to some extent tempered by treatment.

Second, involvement in treatment allows addicts time to think about their future. They are afforded some opportunity, often in a less harried environment than that to which they have become accustomed, to "sort out their lives," to decide whether they want to continue to play the street addict role or whether they wish, as Biernacki (1986) has shown, to either resurrect previous identities or develop new ones.

Third, addicts are aided in this process by exposure to others who are not dependent upon drug use as a primary mode of defining their self-identities. Counselors and other treatment personnel are individuals who have either always lived drug abuse-free lives or, as in the case of ex-addict counselors, have demonstrated that they can make the difficult transition to a drug-free life. This interaction with nonaddict others provides important benefits to the street addict. The sheer amount of time spent solely with addicts and others in the life is significantly reduced. The addict talks and hears about things other than drugs and the drug life. His or her attention is not totally consumed by the drug world; more attention can be given to non-street life concerns. Also, the addict has relatively intimate access to role models who have managed either to define their own identities completely outside of drugs or to "rescue" their identities from the drug world. Thus, the street addict in treatment is provided with an opportunity to interact in a prolonged and hopefully meaningful way with a new set of nonaddict significant others. These significant others actively support the idea that the client can leave the street addict way of life. They also may help the addict to shape new identities and roles.

A fourth benefit of treatment is that it may provide the street addict with an opportunity to explore other alternative nonaddict roles. Most treatment programs, especially those supported by public monies, offer a panoply of ancillary services which may assist the addict to develop new roles. Two examples of such services are the academic and vocational training efforts provided directly or indirectly by many treatment programs. Entry into virtually any meaningful job opportunity today in America requires that the person possess at the minimum a high school diploma. Because of the educational disadvantages most street addicts endure, they are "shut out" of most jobs. From a role-theoretic perspective, they are denied the opportunity to play those roles, because they do not possess the basic minimal entry requirements. Not only do most street addicts lack formal academic credentials, they often lack any other "legitimate" job skills or habits necessary for the attainment and holding of a job. The educational and vocational training services (including efforts at inculcating work-related values such as regular and punctual attendance at the work site) offered by many treatment programs provide addicts with an opportunity to enhance and broaden their skills so that roles previously unavailable to them may become open to them in the future.

These, then, are some of the common attributes that many treatment programs share whatever their own individual and different therapeutic philosophies. We shall now turn to a discussion of these individual philosophies. In doing so, I shall first describe the general outline of the modality. Then, using the sociocultural perspective as a guide, I shall evaluate the program noting both its strengths and weaknesses.

Methadone Maintenance

One of the principal modalities used to treat narcotic addicts in the United States today is methadone maintenance. The original theoretical basis for methadone maintenance is the metabolic deficiency theory, a physiologically based explanation for addiction. Originally posited by Dole and Nyswander (1980), this theory argues that some persons who regularly use narcotics undergo a metabolic or neurological transformation such that they must continue to use narcotics. The analogy is often made to diabetes. The diabetic, because of a metabolic deficiency, must take insulin in order to live. Similarly, because of a metabolic deficiency, addicts must continue to take narcotics to function normally.

I am not really certain of the status of the metabolic deficiency theory among the practitioners of methadone maintenance today. Certainly there is no conclusive laboratory evidence to support it. Contrary to what the theory might predict, it is known that many thousands of addicts have been able to give up their habits. While many early adherents of this modality probably thought of methadone maintenance as possibly a lifelong treatment, current Federal guidelines discourage such a viewpoint. Programs are directed to attempt to withdraw clients from methadone within two years of being stabilized on the drug.

Whatever the status of its theoretical underpinning, methadone maintenance programming usually works in the following way. There are three stages of treatment: stabilization, maintenance, and detoxification. When the addict presents himself for treatment, medical personnel make a determination of the size of the individual's street habit. If the habit is not too large (and typically habits are not that large anymore), the addict is gradually brought up to and stabilized on a fairly low methadone dosage. Often addicts are stabilized at a daily dose below 35 mg although clients may receive as much as 100 mg or more of methadone per day. Determination of the size of the dose is based primarily on the idea that the addict should be addicted to methadone at a level high enough that sufficient cross-tolerance to other narcotics is established. If the addict is effectively stabilized, a challenge to that cross-tolerance with heroin or some other narcotic, under normal circumstances, would be unsuccessful. Put simply, if the addict tries to get high on heroin after receiving his or her dose of methadone, nothing will happen. In popular parlance the methadone has "blocked" the euphoric effects of the heroin.[1]

Then, for the better part of the time the client is on the program, he or she receives this maintenance dose (which may be adjusted upwards or downwards in consultation with treatment personnel). While the client is receiving this maintenance dose, federal regulations require that other treatment services also be provided directly or through referral. These may include individual or group counseling (for the client's underlying emotional problems), medical treatment, educational or vocational guidance, job placement, and a number of other social services. Finally, the day arrives when the counselors and/or medical personnel decide that the client must be presented with the option of withdrawing from methadone. Usually, if the client agrees, the process is a slow and carefully thought out one. The dosage level is gradually reduced so as to minimize any discomfort to the client. Hopefully, at some point the client can become totally drug-free and lead a productive life without the need for chemicals.

While there are many criticisms of methadone maintenance, the chief one is the fact that one narcotic is simply substituted for another. As seen in Chapter 1, methadone is indeed a narcotic. In fact, it is a particularly potent one requiring only one oral dose per day to stave off withdrawal. Contrast this to the three daily doses of heroin typically needed to avoid withdrawal. (Indeed, there is a more powerful form of the drug 1-alpha acetylmethadol—LAAM which is used once every three days. In this country it was used experimentally for a while in maintenance programs and appeared to be reasonably successful.)

However, the fact that methadone is a narcotic has caused much criticism and, at times, outrage. Critics question the wisdom of simply substituting one powerfully addictive substance for another. Others, who speak with more strident voices, contend that methadone maintenance is immoral and simply chemically enslaves its clients. Almost all agree that the provision of methadone in and of itself does not deal with the underlying cause of the addiction. Back in the sixties, when methadone maintenance first came to national prominence, acrimonious battle lines were drawn around this issue. I am happy to report that the fervor of those long gone days has cooled, and the arguments—both pro and con—have become somewhat more tempered.

By and large, I should say "up front" that I have a bias in favor of the modality, although some of my early work on methadone diversion was interpreted by its adherents as extremely hostile. It seems to me that methadone maintenance, as contrasted with other modalities alone, is required to take the most difficult cases to treat. Because federal regulations require that potential clients must demonstrate a history of narcotic addiction, it is almost certainly true that the modality receives more than its fair share of truly hard-core and committed street addicts. Thus, in many ways the modality has the deck stacked against it when comparing its treatment success rates with other modalities.

From a sociocultural perspective, I believe that there are both pros and cons as regards methadone maintenance. Let's first look at its more positive aspects. In many ways, methadone maintenance initially demands less of the clients than do some of the other modalities. This is because the modality does not mandate that addicts give up a central aspect of their lives, namely the use of narcotics.[2] In fact, the narcotic remains a meaningful part of the addicts' lives. The daily ritual of seeking and using a narcotic continues, although in the admittedly more sterile and less exciting environment of a treatment clinic. The "chemical crutch" that the addicts may have remains intact. The drug is still there to support them.[3] Yet at the same time, because they no longer need to "hustle and cop" or need to worry about where their next fix is coming from, they can attend to their therapeutic progress. They may be able to find a job or go to school or in other ways try out or develop new and different roles. But, unlike the commitment demanded by other modalities, addicts need not give up their use of drugs, at least not for a significant period of time.

The very fact of the centrality of the drug itself in methadone maintenance can also be seen as a criticism from the sociocultural viewpoint. It seems to me that the typography of many methadone clinics themselves reinforce what I am talking about. When one enters a clinic, almost invariably within just a few steps of the front door is the methadone dispensing window. The client goes there to receive not only the drug but also any instructions which will be attached to the client's medication card. Administrative and counseling offices are most often off to one side or on a different floor. The drug takes center stage.

Thus, the client is constantly reminded of the central importance of the drug to his or her life. Other aspects of the therapeutic process of leaving the addict role are minimized. Taking of the drug is the only "therapeutic event" that ordinarily occurs every day in the patient's life. The drug is king! Thus, the addict may be convinced, as possibly the individual described in my footnote, that life without the drug is difficult if not impossible.

Self-Help Programs

The Therapeutic Community

Another major genre of treatment program is based on mutual self-help. There are two types of programs: the residential self-help community known as the therapeutic community (t.c.) and the nonresidential Narcotics Anonymous, which operates according to the principles of Alcoholics Anonymous. Generally, the t.c.s oriented to treating narcotic addicts got their start in the early 1950s when Chuck Dederich founded the famous—some might say infamous—Synanon. For quite a while, Synanon served as the model for the many other therapeutic communities that sprouted about the country. Most therapeutic communities still adhere to much of this model, so it might be worth our while to describe the basic outlines of many such programs. First, and foremost, the t.c. philosophy focuses on the concept of self-help. Most early therapeutic communities believed, as does Alcoholics Anonymous, that escape from addiction can be accomplished only through one's own efforts with the assistance of others who have traveled the same pathway. Thus, the communities were all composed of former users (although it is interesting to note that Dederich himself was a former alcoholic and was not a narcotic addict). The use of professionals to provide psychiatric or psychotherapeutic help was prohibited. While many t.c.s now have professional staff, and in some cases are headed by psychiatrists or other mental health professionals, there is still very heavy reliance on the ex-addict as the central "treatment provider" in the organization.

Another hallmark of the philosophy is the belief that the addict is a "baby," a person who is emotionally immature. This individual has never grown up. Accordingly, the junkie has to be taught to "grow up." This principle has several important ramifications in determining the shape and operations of the t.c.; indeed, the whole structure of the "house" is oriented around this principle. Therapeutic communities are usually hierarchically structured with the director at the top of a steep pyramidal structure. At the very bottom of the pyramid are the jobs that require the least skill and are the most unattractive. These jobs include the most menial tasks such as cleaning the bathroom or washing the dishes. As one climbs the organizational ladder, one takes on increasingly more important responsibilities while at the same time enjoying more perquisites.

Another ramification of the belief in the immaturity of the addict is the fact that life in the community is highly structured. A rigorously defined schedule is adhered to in the community. From the moment residents wake to the time they go to sleep, they know what they are supposed to be doing. They need only consult the house schedule to know what is to happen at any time.

In addition to a strict timetable, the house also possesses an elaborate set of rules governing all aspects of life. The house member knows what is "right" and "wrong" with almost any kind of behavior that can occur in the house. Attached to the rules are penalties. In the "old days" major rule infractions could be punished by haircuts (sometimes literally shaving the head) or the wearing of diapers to publicly demonstrate one's immaturity.

The "treatment mechanism" which is used to help the addict mature is the "game" or what Synanon originally called the "synanon." Games occur every day in most t.c.s. Indeed, there is often more than one game per day and sometimes there are marathons which are games that last for forty-eight hours or more (usually on weekends). The game is similar to what used to be called "t" or confrontational groups. All members of the house are expected to participate in the game. Indeed, one principle of the game is that anyone, including even the director in some houses, can be called to explain or defend a behavior. Frequently, the transgressions of members of the house are revealed by other members. It is generally expected that members should "inform" on one another.

The game is sometimes utilized to direct attention to one member of the house. Such an individual is put on the "hot seat" and becomes the therapeutic focus of the whole group. For instance, an individual might be asked to explain why he or she is an addict. Offering "excuses" such as use of drugs to cope with stress or assigning blame for one's use on others are vigorously attacked by the group. The member is made to realize that he or she is solely responsible for the use of drugs. From an outsider's viewpoint, these sessions can become quite brutal reducing the targeted person to a crying, anguished, and pitiable "mess." Such sessions invariably end, however, with all members hugging and expressing love for one another.

The whole structure of the house then is centered about the "socialization" of the immature addict into a responsible adult. Because newly arrived junkies are seen to be immature, they are assigned menial tasks and are supervised closely. Slowly, over time, if they demonstrate trustworthiness and increasing maturity, they gradually move up the pyramid. From a role perspective, they are given increasingly more complex and more important roles to play. However, at any time, should individuals "slide" back into behaving or thinking like a street junkie, they can be demoted to a lower level. For very severe infractions (the use of drugs, violence, or the threat of violence) members can be expelled from the community.

Needless to say, the therapeutic community experience is a powerful one. The heavy reliance on an absolute hierarchy and an all encompassing set of rules has led to some horrible abuses.[4] In response, many therapeutic communities employ trained treatment professionals as house directors. Others, while still eschewing the use of professionals, appoint boards of directors or trustees who are drawn from the larger community. Such businessmen, community professionals, and other lay persons keep a close watch on the fiscal and other operations of the house.

As one might imagine, the therapeutic community concept has attracted both severe critics and ardent defenders. Some of the critics have focused on the abuses which have commonly occurred in the past. Others note that the approach is extremely expensive, given the fact that persons are typically expected to reside in the community for a minimum of two years. Some opponents point out that the approach appeals to a notably small number of addicts. Ordinarily, fewer than ten percent of all admissions remain in the modality for the requisite time period.

Yet another criticism is that few of the successfully treated members of the community ever "graduate," that is leave the house to lead a "normal life" on the outside. Stung by this criticism, many houses now concentrate on reintegrating their members into the community. Other t.c.s, however, believe either that their lifestyle is superior to that on the outside or that members should be given the choice of whether they want to graduate or not. Some t.c.s have, to some meaningful extent, become alternative, almost utopian, communities whose members plan to live their whole lives within the community. I know of one such t.c. where a couple, who initially had to request the community's permission to marry, are raising their children in a type of "communalistic" environment according to the precepts of the community.[5]

How can we view the pros and cons of this approach from the perspective of the role theory proposed in this book? Well, it is certainly clear that the whole process of "treating" the addict fits within the role perspective proffered here, for the experience which a junkie undergoes in the therapeutic community is essentially a dramatic example of adult socialization. The individual is ripped from a world in which there is a whole set of deviant norms, values, and role expectations and placed into another environment which is in many ways the exact opposite of the previous existence. The individual is expected to act in a prescribed way, and any return to the values or behaviors of the previous life are severely devalued and punished.

It is not surprising that so few street addicts are able to "stick it out" in a therapeutic community. From the sociocultural perspective, there are a number of reasons for the "failure" of the t.c. with most junkies. First, as noted above, the decidedly "square" values of the therapeutic community (with emphasis on punctuality, hard work, trust and belief in others, and complete abstinence from all psychoactive substances, with the notable exceptions of nicotine and caffeine) run counter to the most dearly held beliefs of the street addict. Secondly, addicts, who previously saw themselves as the coolest of the cool, must now accept an abased definition of self as a "child." Third, unlike methadone maintenance which, through its provision of another narcotic helps "bridge" the transition from one role to another, the therapeutic community offers no such help. In fact, many t.c.s insist on "cold turkey withdrawal," further testing the sincerity and mettle of the admittees. Thus, the transition may be too abrupt for all but those most committed to their quest for a drug-free life.

It appears, however, that the therapeutic community does work well for some individuals. This should not be surprising when viewed from the sociocultural perspective. As noted, what goes on in the therapeutic community is actually a form of extreme adult socialization (or re-socialization, if you prefer). First, addicts are stripped almost totally of their current identities. A new and very carefully defined "self" is substituted. A new set of significant others is created for the individual. (Many therapeutic communities do not allow new admittees to have any interaction with family or other former significant others. Even after residents have been in the house for some time, their contact with "outsiders" is often still tightly controlled.) Virtually all interaction with these new significant others is based on degradation or stigmatization of the old identity while at the same time reinforcing the new one. Rule transgressions are seen as indicators of immature "junkie" behavior while approved behaviors are rewarded with praise and promotion within the house hierarchy. In short, the person is socialized into a new "square" identity.

Narcotics Anonymous

As I noted in the beginning of this section, yet another type of self-help program is Narcotics Anonymous, which is based on the famous Twelve Steps method of Alcoholics Anonymous. This model presents an interesting paradox. It requires the addict to admit that he is hopelessly habituated to a drug and that he can never, not even once, use that drug again. In a certain way, this almost seems to "trap" the individual into a deviant identity. Yet at the same time, Narcotics Anonymous presents another role identity—that of the recovering addict. A principal tenet of the organization is that the addict is always only one "shot" away from failure. Yet with the help of friends who constantly reaffirm the new identity of "recovering addict," the individual can lead a new and drug-free life.

There are both ardent proponents and critics of the Narcotics/ Alcoholics Anonymous approach. It is clear that some persons benefit from the approach. In fact, it appears that the Alcoholics Anonymous philosophy has enjoyed a new wave of popularity with many residential and nonresidential treatment programs incorporating the A.A. approach. In fact, it is so popular that it has almost taken on the dimensions of a social movement. And, of course, many of its members swear by the efficacy of the approach. It has become something akin to a religion to some of its members. Indeed the spiritual aspects of the method are central to its philosophy.

There are also a number of criticisms of the approach. In fact, critics seem to have become more verbal recently. One controversial critique is provided by Fingarette (1988). Both he and Peele (1985) have criticized the "disease model" (especially the viewpoint that alcoholism and drug abuse may be genetically based diseases) that seems to have been so fervently embraced by many A.A. supporters. The extent of the success which A.A. claims has also never been firmly established. The organization has effectively avoided evaluation utilizing tightly designed control studies. I, along with others, also doubt the wisdom of "selling" the viewpoint that even one drop of alcohol or drug almost certainly means relapse to a former and less desirable state. Alcoholics Anonymous has been singularly effective in spreading the idea in the treatment community that return to social drinking (and presumably controlled substance use) is an impossibility for the addicted person. Yet, Fingarette (1988) points out that the evidence in support of this position is tenuous, at best, and that this "truth" is much less firmly accepted in the European treatment and research communities. What troubles me most is that a person who "buys" into this goal of total and complete abstinence is almost pre-ordained to failure if he or she slips up.

In summary, whether the person is a member of a therapeutic community or of Alcoholics/Narcotics Anonymous, it is clear that recovery can be understood from the sociocultural perspective. Basically, abstinence results from: intense adult socialization; interaction with a new group of "significant others" who are themselves recovered addicts; the debasement of a prior identity; and great social reward for enactment of a new non-addict role and self-identity.

Other Treatment Approaches

Outpatient Treatment Programs

There are a number of other treatment approaches. Probably the most common treatment modality today is simply a type of out patient program which views the individual as suffering from a type of emotional illness of which drug abuse is only a symptom. Almost all schools of psychological or psychoanalytic thought find representation in these programs. Some have very focused treatment philosophies, while others are eclectic. Typically they utilize some form of professionally oriented psychological treatment. Such programs include a combination of individual counseling and group therapy. Clients are also often provided other types of services, either directly or through referral. Vocational counseling, educational programs, and assistance to clients in wending their way through health care, welfare, and other public and semi-private bureaucracies is often provided.

It is difficult to critique these programs from the sociocultural perspective, because they are so heterogeneous and have so many different foci. Their philosophies and methods of treatment often are not as coherent as those found in methadone maintenance and self-help programs. They are probably most helpful when they can provide "assistance" to the well-motivated client in the transition from the addict to nonaddict identity. The decision to give up drugs and the addict lifestyle is a difficult one, and it is useful to have individuals who are there to help in that decision and be supportive. Equally important is having a person who can marshall the forces of the community to support an individual, in both tangible and emotional ways, in that decision. Many outpatient programs can provide such needed support.

Detoxification programs

Many facilities in the United States also provide detoxification from drugs, either as part of an integrated program of services or as a stand-alone service. Most often these programs keep the patient for only a few weeks. These are the least successful of programs, and the sociocultural perspective explains why (Simpson and Sells, 1981). Basically, detoxification is too centered on the physiological aspects of drug addiction. While it would not be fair to say that these programs ignore the other sociological and psychological aspects of addiction, their principal goal is simply to break the person's physiological dependence on the chemical substance. Because of the brief time that clients are with them, they often do not have time to deal with the nonphysiological aspects. Certainly, their treatment is not lengthy enough to induce the slow changes in self-concept and behavior called for by both the sociocultural and psychological perspectives. Their sole role, it would seem to me, is to help break a physiological dependency on a drug so that a person who is otherwise committed to developing a new lifestyle will not have to worry about where the next "fix" is coming from.

The Sociocultural Perspective and Treatment Philosophies

Throughout this chapter we have looked at various treatment modalities and explored their underlying treatment philosophies. I have critiqued the approaches from the sociocultural perspective. While I know of no treatment program which utilizes the sociocultural perspective to guide its treatment regimen, I think most programs cannot ignore the realities posed by the sociocultural approach. I feel there are certain treatment-related principles which derive from the sociocultural approach and can be useful to counselors and other treatment personnel. Among these are the following:

1. One does not need to view heroin addicts as "sick" individuals.

This has been an underlying principle throughout this book. I believe that many treatment programs are on the "wrong track" when they view substance abuse as a physiological or emotional disease (or symptom of a mental disease). In a certain way it makes individuals more helpless and less responsible for their own behavior. It often puts the responsibility for the treatment in the hands of the provider. After all, one goes to the doctor when one is ill. If the patient does not get well, it may be an open question as to whether that is the fault of the patient or the treatment.[6]

Rather, the sociocultural approach views addiction as the result of a commitment to a lifestyle. The role is slowly assumed by individuals and, to a certain extent, is rationally chosen by them. Therefore individuals must accept at least a part of the responsibility for changing their self-concepts and role behaviors.

2. The addict role must be viewed within a larger social and cultural context.

That is not to say that the street addict is solely responsible for his or her own behavior. For this truly would be a classic case of blaming the victim, at least in the case of most heroin addicts in America today. Clearly, it is not coincidental that most heroin use and intravenous abuse of other drugs appears in the most disadvantaged neighborhoods of this country. To demand that addicts change and pull themselves up by their own bootstraps is unrealistic and unfair.

The society must provide the resources for addicts to leave the lifestyle. This means that access to meaningful educational and vocational opportunities must be provided by the society. And treatment programs need to become more skilled in shepherding addicts through the massive and dehumanizing human service bureaucracies which ostensibly exist to serve such clients. We must never lose sight of the fact that addicts can be expected to adopt new roles only if reasonably attractive and existentially meaningful new roles are made available to them.

3. Resocialization and adoption of new roles is a slow and arduous task.

Many street addicts have spent years in that role. In fact, for many of them it may be the only adult role which they have played or which they have performed with any degree of proficiency. As we have seen, a fundamental sense of self-identification and self-worth is tied up in this role. Combine with this the fact that the addict may lack the skills to play other roles. Or, if the addict does possess the skills to play other roles, access to these may be blocked because of social class or racial bias. Indeed, knowledge by others of persons' past histories as addicts can block access to "legitimate" work and social order.

Thus, one should not expect treatment to change the individual overnight. The process will probably be a long and painful one. It may well be a process of two steps forward and one step backwards. Nevertheless, treatment programs should be there to provide emotional and other types of support for this existential journey, no matter how interrupted the trip.

4. Relapse is an expectable phenomenon.

Part of this interruption will no doubt include relapse. We should expect this. Indeed, some treatment personnel define addiction as a chronic relapsing condition. Remember that an intimate component of an addict's identity is use of drugs. Accordingly, it is the rare case where the addict can completely and abruptly substitute a nonaddict identity for an addict identity. As noted above, the process of re-socialization is a slow one and it is to be expected that "slips" back into previous self-definitions will occur while new identities are forged.

Many programs expel addicts if they reuse drugs. For some there is virtually no tolerance for drug use (as in some therapeutic communities), while others permit some use if it does not become too frequent. I feel that programs need to be rather generous in allowing clients to abuse drugs, especially if such clients have only recently attempted to give up the addict lifestyle. Clearly, if there is evidence that the relapsed client is simply "using" the program, then expulsion may be indicated. However, I do not believe that relapse is necessarily an indicator that either the client or the program has failed. It may simply be due to the fact that relapse is an expectable part of most attempts at abstinence.

5. Treatment will work only with committed clients.

There is no "magic bullet" in the treatment of narcotics addicts. I guess partially because of the hegemony of the disease and medical models, we could expect that much effort is devoted to finding a physiologically based cure for addiction—the so-called magic bullet. After all, a patient can often be cured with drugs whether or not he has a conscious desire to be cured. Unfortunately, in my view, the same does not hold true for addiction. It seems to me that an addict can be "cured" only if he or she has a conscious desire to give up drugs. I suspect that most drug treatment programs are not overly successful with their clients because of this elementary fact. Many persons who are in treatment may be there because of legal or other kinds of pressures external to them. They are not genuinely interested in giving up the drug life or drug use. Treatment for these non-motivated individuals simply does not make sense.

6. *More conscious attention needs to be paid to the sociocultural aspects of drug abuse.*

While most treatment personnel are aware of the realities of the street life, I do not believe there is enough conscious attention paid to the kinds of issues outlined in this book. First, treatment personnel must more fully take into account the magnetic pull of the subculture. They must realize the enormous influence that addict significant others have on addicts in treatment. The temptation to relapse is always there and it is fueled by addict friends who encourage clients to "go back to the cooker." Treatment strategies need to be developed which help clients to "insulate" themselves from such pressure. Often this might include moving the person out of the old drug using neighborhood so as to put physical distance between clients and their old environments.

Treatment personnel also need to realize the salience of the addict self-image to the clients. Self esteem is built on the clients view of themselves as being "cool." While therapy might have to challenge, indeed destroy, this self-image, it is imperative that a new self-image be substituted for the old one. Otherwise, the client, out of a desire for some self-respect or dignity, may well return to the old street addict role.

Finally, treatment personnel need to be cognizant of the very real structural limits under which most street addicts live. Because of social and economic barriers erected by both social class and racial discrimination, many addicts are restricted from entering a number of "legitimate" societal roles. While these factors go far beyond what the typical treatment program can impact on, treatment personnel must be cognizant of the fact that they cannot "set up" their clients to fail through setting unreasonably high goals for them. For these and many other reasons, treatment will invariably be a slow and tortuous process characterized as much by failure as success.

At any rate, treatment is only one of the many remedies which has been offered for solution of the drug problem in America. In the next chapter, I shall review a number of other proposals offered in the search for a solution.

Chapter Eight

What Is To Be Done

In this final chapter, I shall briefly review the various strategies which have been proposed to deal with the "drug crisis" in America. Probably the most prominent of these revolves around dealing with the problem through legal processes. These proposals range all the way from heavy penalties for use or sale of drugs (including capital punishment) to coerced treatment for targeted populations. Yet others have advocated the establishment of heroin maintenance programs in the United States. More benign legally oriented proposals call for the legalization or at least decriminalization of certain types of drugs. I shall now review these various proposals by first describing and critiquing each of them.

Harsher Penalties and Stricter Enforcement

Since the beginning of the Reagan administration, the United States has seen the war on drugs become a prime public and political issue. Indeed, the war seems to have escalated in the Bush administration, with the resultant enlargement of anti-drug efforts at the federal level. While much rhetoric has been bantered about concerning the enlargement of drug treatment slots, it is clear that enforcement of current and possibly even harsher laws in the future will take center stage in this campaign.

Over the last several years, in particular, there has been a subtle change in the criminal justice community from "supply side" to the "demand side enforcement strategies." That is, many government and law enforcement officials argue that the only way ultimately to cope with the problem is to go after the buyers. If there is no demand, they reason, dealers will have no one to whom they can sell their drugs.

Pursuant to this policy, many police departments are "sweeping" neighborhoods in which drugs are sold. Both sellers and users are netted; large numbers of persons are arrested. Some police officials feel that only by applying this kind of pressure can both the dealer and the seller be made aware that real penalties will be attached to their actions. Indeed, one large city police chief recently said that drug users, as well as sellers, are traitors to their country and should legally be dealt with as such. He was unconcerned that "buyers" might be caught up in an arrest net. He felt that severe penalties, including seizure of property such as automobiles was warranted. He felt by making examples of a few individuals the word would go out that purchase of drugs was too risky an enterprise in which to engage.

Combined with increased surveillance and arrest activities, there has been renewed discussion of harsher penalties for both users and sellers. Indeed, capital punishment has been proposed for certain types of high-level, "kingpin" types of drug dealers. And there have been recent calls for more stringent penalties attached to almost all levels of use.

How can one view these proposals from the sociocultural perspective? It is a difficult question to answer. If one has bought my argument all along that heroin and other psychoactive drug use is to some extent a rational activity, then presumably addicts must weigh the rewards and costs of their drug use activities. Using this reasoning, when the financial, legal, or social costs of addiction outweigh its rewards, persons will stop using drugs. I believe that addicts can and indeed do engage in this type of reasoning. The reasons that persons enter treatment or try on their own to give up drugs are often related to the intolerable costs associated with use. Addicts may check themselves into drug treatment programs because they have reached the "greasy dope fiend" stage and their habits can no longer be maintained. They are embarrassed about their inability to project the proper kind of cool image. Hence, they will try to detox so they can begin to reuse at a more reasonable and less costly level. Similarly, others simply tire of the addict life-style and make efforts to adopt other less costly and more reward-ing roles.

Thus, if the costs of continuing to use become too great, one could expect that many addicts will simply stop using. The costs may be either direct legal penalties (i.e. imprisonment) or indirect (i.e. the increased costs of drugs due to shortages brought about by intense enforcement efforts). I believe that should such a situation really occur, we probably would see a genuine decline in drug use. But it would take a comprehensive, expensive, and long-term commitment by government at all levels for this situation to occur. And it would take a long time for addicts to finally realize the costs of their addiction.

Let's first look more closely at this latter point. Most of us have this view of addiction as being a high-risk activity. And, to a certain extent, that is true. But it is nowhere as legally risky as one would presume. First, there is the fact that addicts are rarely caught for their criminal activities. In fact, Inciardi and Chambers (1972) demonstrated long ago that addicts are caught for only about one percent of the crimes they commit. And excluded from this definition of crime is use or possession of drugs in and of itself! Thus, the addict does not live in constant fear of arrest.

But even more so, once arrested, drug users often do not fear dire consequences. The statistics bear this out. The Drug Use Forecasting Project (DUF), funded by the National Institute of Justice, is a research program designed to estimate the extent of psychoactive drug use in a sample of recent arrestees. Persons who have been charged largely with non-drug felonies (robbery, theft, murder, etc.) are interviewed and voluntarily give anonymous urine samples within forty-eight hours of arrest. Data from this project, which operates in a number of large cities in the United States, indicate that from 54 percent to 82 percent of male arrestees test positive for some psychoactive drug (National Institute of Justice, 1989). Many of these individuals are probably fairly habitual users. Presently, there simply are not enough jail or prison cells in this country to hold the large numbers of inmates that would be produced should drug laws be strictly enforced. The costs of constructing and operating enough prisons to contain all these individuals are beyond economic reality. I believe most addicts know these facts through their own experiences with the criminal justice system. Plea bargaining, placement on probation or parole, and other mechanisms are used to reduce both the number of people who serve time and the length of their sentences.

In the final analysis, then, I believe addicts realize that the legal costs of their drug use are relatively low, given the rewards of the lifestyle. Conversely, the costs to the society of truly enforcing stricter laws might be unacceptably great.

I believe we can see that incarceration of large numbers of drug users, as indicated by the DUF data, would be prohibitively expensive and probably impossibly so. But more importantly, the costs to the very fabric of American life would be too great. Here I am referring to the assault on the Bill of Rights that would almost certainly occur in the enforcement of stricter laws. Already suggestions have come from some quarters to reduce civil liberties in cases where drug law violations are suspected. Some have suggested that the need for a search warrant be abandoned in suspected drug cases. We have already seen the seizure of private property in some drug cases including impoundment of pleasure boats when small quantities of drugs, including remnants of a marihuana cigarette, were found. And the press has documented cases where drug agents invaded the homes of innocent people in the middle of the night because violation of drug laws were suspected. There have even been suggestions that the military be used to *enforce* drug laws in local communities. While the military already plays a role in drug interdiction at the borders of the United States, this would be a new and, in my opinion, potentially ominous use for soldiers. Imagine the specter of federal troops patrolling your neighborhood.

The spillover of concern about the drug problem into American life has begun to occur. Already we see more and more employers in both the private and public sectors demanding urine testing both for potential and current employees. I view this as an unpardonable invasion of privacy. Certainly, I believe no employer has the right to tell you what you can do on your off hours. The chief concern should be whether your behavior on the job is appropriate. Unless there is probable cause, employers should not have the right to routinely screen all their employees. The danger of allowing employers to govern off-job behavior could easily be expanded to include not only one's substance use but organizations to which one can belong. The dangers to precious civil liberties are real. But beyond this is the pitiful image of Americans lining up at their workplace to be observed as they fill their urine sample bottles.

I do not have the space here to analyze this issue in depth. However, an important book has recently been written on the subject. It is Arnold Trebach's *The Great Drug War* (1987), which details the threats to American civil liberties. It is "must" reading for someone who wants to be informed about the issue.

I guess another reason I have such doubts about the efficacy of stricter law enforcement is because it seems that we have been down this path so many times before. There is little doubt that the "drug problem" has worsened since the passage of the Harrison Act in 1917. Since that time more and more laws have been enacted at all levels of government attempting to control drugs and "criminalizing" those who use them. From a broader historical perspective, then, as these laws have proliferated, the problem of drug use has increased. While this point obviously glosses over enormous political and social changes in the last seven decades, it is nevertheless true that more and harsher laws have neither effectively eliminated nor possibly even limited the drug problem.

Harsher law enforcement probably got its most effective test in the early 1970s in New York State upon passage of the so-called Rockefeller laws. Sales of drugs were heavily penalized. For example, sale of one ounce of heroin could bring a sentence of fifteen years to life; this was the same penalty as provided for premeditated murder. Judicial discretion in sentencing was limited in certain instances. Yet for a variety of reasons discussed elsewhere (Stephens, 1987), the experiment failed. The harsher laws simply did not work.

Coerced Treatment

Many observers have concluded the creation of statutes outlawing drugs and rather broad enforcement of these laws does not appear to work. One such individual, John Kaplan in *The Hardest Drug* (1983), has proposed that the laws be strenuously targeted at those individuals whose drug use is most disruptive to the society. He believes that there are many individuals whose drug use constitutes a threat only to themselves and not to the general fabric of the society. The legal establishment should more or less ignore these persons. Instead, law enforcement efforts ought to be aimed at those addicts who account for such large amounts of street crime. Rather than incarcerate these individuals, however, they should be given a choice: treatment or jail. While Kaplan acknowledges treatment has not been shown to be terribly effective, at least persons might slowly be weaned from their habits and street addict behaviors.

I believe that Kaplan's suggestion is borne of mild desperation. Kaplan develops his solution after an exhaustive and scholarly rejection of other options including stricter law enforcement, interdiction, legalization, and other options. It is almost like he listed all of the possible options and then felt that his coerced treatment was the least objectionable, all things considered.

There are a number of difficulties with Kaplan's plan. As I have noted elsewhere (Stephens, 1987), I believe that coerced treatment has been tried previously. For a review of coerced treatment see Leukefeld and Tims (1988). Indeed, the intellectual justification for the approach is found in Brill and Lieberman's *Authority and Addiction* (1969), wherein it is argued that addicts are emotionally ill individuals who need help. They lack self-control and therefore need to be supervised by therapists until they have become well. The basis of this control rested in the therapists' professional knowledge and treatment tools. As it takes time to treat this difficult disease, therapists need to be able to maintain physical control over their clients so that their patients will continue to show up for treatment. In Brill and Lieberman's terms, the therapists should exercise "rational authority" over their clients.

This idea eventually developed into what were called "civil commitment" programs and became very popular in the late 1960s. Both California and New York had large civil commitment programs. The Federal government also seized upon the idea and the Narcotic Addict Rehabilitation Act of 1968 (NARA) embodied most of the provisions of a civil commitment program. While the act was rather complex, basically it stipulated that addicts could volunteer to civilly commit themselves under the NARA treatment program. The treatment program had two major components: a six month inpatient phase followed by aftercare in the community. Detoxification, assessment, and initial treatment were accomplished at one of the two federal narcotics treatment hospitals (at Lexington, Kentucky, and Fort Worth, Texas). Following the six months of inpatient treatment, clients were assigned to an aftercare counselor to whom they were required to report on a weekly basis. The unique aspect of the NARA was its civil commitment provisions. Once clients civilly committed themselves, they lost the right to check themselves out of the hospital "against medical advice" and, should their aftercare counselor so determine, they could be returned to the hospital for additional treatment.

It should be noted that most of these clients were exactly the type that Kaplan feels should be coerced into treatment. They were typical street addicts. Even though they were civil commitments, the fact of the matter was that most were there under some sort of legal pressure. Typically, they faced a situation where a state or local judge gave them the option of either going to jail or going to Lexington. While Lexington was no bed of roses (being fundamentally a prison-type hospital), it sure beat most federal and state prisons.

Yet civil commitment seems to have largely been a failure. (There are exceptions; see Leukefeld [1988].) Like almost all narcotic addict treatment programs, relapse was observed for large numbers of its clients (Stephens and Cottrell, 1972). Then, too, the programs were very expensive. At the federal level two large hospitals and a large network of aftercare counselors, whose caseloads were designed to be atypically low, had to be maintained. It must be said, too, that many clients simply absconded from aftercare.

Since I was a researcher employed by the Lexington, Kentucky, facility for some of the time that NARA was in effect, I believe I was able to get an appreciation of the program not only from the perspective of a staff member but, through my contacts with patients, also from the view of those civilly committed. As with most aspects of life, the addicts viewed the program through the lenses of the street addict role. As noted above, most came to the hospital not because they were sincerely interested in giving up dope but because they wanted to beat some "hard time" in prison. Almost all knew that they would go back to using drugs as soon as they "hit the streets" again. Much of their time at the hospital was spent in "conning" staff, especially in attempts to earn early discharge from the hospital (Levine and Stephens, 1972). When in aftercare, they developed strategies to "beat" the urine tests in order to avoid the recommitment that might result from too many positive tests (Stephens and Weppner, 1973B). In short, for most patients, the motivation was to evade the system, not to be cured.

Consequently, these types of programs have largely been abandoned. Besides the practical problem that they did not appear to be any more effective than less expensive programs such as methadone maintenance, I have always been concerned about the civil liberties issues involved. I personally do not believe that mental health and drug treatment professionals have the sophisticated diagnostic knowledge or effective treatment tools to determine which kinds of clients can benefit from civil commitment programs. To invest some human beings with the power to detain other individuals (not convicted of crimes) against their will is a serious business. While I believe the state has the right to do so for persons who have been tried and convicted, to regularize this practice as an administrative function of a court (and allied mental health professionals) presents genuine threats to the civil liberties of all.

In the final analysis, then, I believe that coerced treatment has had "its day in court." While I suppose it can be argued that it is more benign than incarceration without treatment, I believe the record will show that it is no more effective than other approaches. And the potential for abuse of the civil commitment power, especially given America's current political climate, is great.

Interdiction

Over the past eight years, a favorite strategy developed by the Reagan administration for dealing with the drug problem is interdiction. Interdiction is a supply-side strategy. Basically, the argument goes that if supplies of drugs can be effectively halted at America's borders, then there will be much less drug to use, and America will have taken a long step towards solving its drug problem. James Inciardi (1986) reinforces the belief that interdiction is a much needed component of a unified offensive against drug abuse. He also argues that countries such as Columbia which export huge amounts of drugs into this country should be denied American foreign aid.

I have always had great difficulty in understanding the strategy of interdiction. Most of this difficulty rests on what appears to me to be its impracticality. First, there is the issue that small quantities of some drugs such as cocaine or heroin are needed to feed America's habits. One kilogram or 2.2 pounds of heroin or cocaine, easily smuggled by one person into this country, produces thousands of fixes and is worth hundreds of thousands if not millions of dollars on the streets. The economic incentive to take risks in smuggling is simply overwhelming. Second, the border area of the United States is huge. I doubt that all the police forces, including the military, could effectively patrol this vast area. Third, almost all drugs can either be grown or produced here in the United States. Marihuana, for instance, has become a major cash crop in certain parts of the country such as northern California. Other drugs, not easily produced here, have synthetic analogues (such as Phentanyl in place of heroin or "ice" in place of "crack") that can be produced in clandestine labs. Fourth, interdiction efforts may actually create a more difficult to control drug trade than currently exists. When large drug distribution cartels are destroyed through intelligence networks and concerted raids, the danger is that drug distribution may become more diffused to smaller operations making the gathering of enforcement intelligence even more difficult. Finally, there are the civil liberties issues. I believe there is real danger in involving the military in the enforcement of criminal law to any significant degree. To do so would invest the professional military with powers they have not ordinarily had in American society.

Heroin Maintenance

Through the years there has been a call in America for a more medically oriented approach to heroin addiction. Typically, critics of the American way of dealing with heroin use point to the so-called British system. In Britain, all physicians are allowed to prescribe heroin for the treatment of illnesses other than addiction. For instance, a British physician can prescribe a cough syrup that contains heroin. As part of the medical solution to addiction, a network of treatment clinics have been set up around the United Kingdom. In these clinics, and only in these clinics, specially trained physicians are allowed to prescribe heroin for maintenance purposes. That is, a person who has been certified and registered as a narcotic addict may receive maintenance dosages of heroin; there is no requirement that the drug be used for detoxification only.

Probably the most vocal advocate for heroin maintenance in this country is Arnold Trebach. In his book *The Heroin Solution* he calls for an even more radical approach than is currently practiced in Britain. Remember that in the United States today, the use of heroin by any physician, except in the rare research study, is completely proscribed. Trebach argues that *all* American doctors be given the right to prescribe heroin both for the treatment of disease and suffering (as in its use in the Brompton's cocktail for terminally ill patients) and for "treatment of heroin addicts." That is, all addicts would be allowed to go to their family physicians, receive prescriptions for heroin and have these prescriptions filled at the local pharmacy. The decision of when, if ever, to withdraw the client from heroin, would be between the physician and the patient.

Other advocates of heroin maintenance are not quite as "liberal" as Trebach; they argue for a system much more like the traditional

British system. They would like to see clinics established where specially trained doctors and staff would treat addicts. They would be allowed to prescribe heroin for maintenance purposes in much the same way as methadone is prescribed today. In fact, except for the drug being used for maintenance, I imagine the programs would appear to be almost identical.

One can see the advantages of a heroin maintenance system. It would make heroin—an intrinsically inexpensive drug—incredibly cheap by today's illegal marketplace standards. It would also insure that addicts are getting drugs of assured quality. By making the drug so cheap, it would probably destroy the drug's distribution and sales networks. Street crime would probably be significantly reduced since so much of it is driven by the price of drugs. It is even possible that disruption of the drug distribution network might lead to fundamental changes in the street addict way of life such that the subculture, so heavily dependent on the centrality of the drug, would disappear.

Yet there are many criticisms of this plan. As with methadone maintenance, one can claim that by providing a drug on a mainten- ance basis, one is treating only the symptoms of the "disease." The underlying root causes are not being dealt with. (It seems that this criticism might be applicable only to a program which simply pro- vided heroin and no other ancillary services.) Others argue that one is simply enslaving the person to a drug and such bondage is not morally justifiable.

Yet another problem is diversion of heroin into a hitherto nonusing population. It is clear that diversion of methadone from maintenance programs was a major problem in the past (Inciardi, 1977). If heroin is dispensed by physicians all over the country, the potential is certainly there for it to "get out" into the general population. While diversion can be more controlled in a clinic set- ting, it could not be totally eliminated especially if take-home doses are allowed. Almost certainly, take-home doses would have to be permitted. Imagine the inconvenience to clients should they be required to report to the clinic three times a day seven days a week for long stretches of time. Either the society would have to risk the danger of diversion or impose an almost impossible treat- ment regimen on the patients.

172 THE STREET ADDICT ROLE

Another unknown in heroin maintenance is the ultimate physical costs to the client. Here I am not speaking of the pharmacological dangers of the drug, which as we saw in Chapter 1 are relatively benign. Rather we need to focus on the potential long-term effects of intravenous injection of these drugs thrice daily over long periods of time.

Perhaps some of these reasons have motivated Britain's clinics to move away from heroin maintenance and towards either the use of methadone as the maintenance drug or to total abstinence in the clinic. While Trebach says that such moves are in part due to clinic staff disillusionment with their clients' incessant demands and problems, the above mentioned criticisms of the approach need to be considered as additional reasons for this trend in British programs.

From a sociocultural perspective, I see both pros and cons to the heroin maintenance approach. On a more positive note, I believe that heroin maintenance has all the advantages of methadone maintenance I mentioned in the previous chapter. Most especially, it can act as a bridge into ultimate abstinence or, at least, reduced use. It does not demand total and immediate abstinence. And, at least initially, the novelty of offering heroin in a clinic setting might act as a powerful magnet to attract large numbers of clients into treatment.

But from the sociocultural perspective, I do not believe that the program would ultimately be that much more successful than methadone maintenance. For if the principal theme of this book is correct—namely that persons are addicted to a lifestyle as much as to a substance—then this pharmacological emphasis on a chemical substance is misplaced. It might even be that if heroin became too "respectable," street addict allegiance would be transferred to some other drug such as crack.

In the final analysis, I would argue that heroin maintenance be given an experimental "try" in the United States. (I am positive that investigators will have no shortage of research volunteers.) In fact, the VERA Institute of Justice long ago proposed such a trial. Indeed, in the late 1970s I was approached by a law firm representing some wealthy businessmen who were "tired of the drug problem." They had hired this law firm to explore the possibility of setting up such a program in Texas, and I was asked if I would be involved as one of the researchers. Of course, I jumped at the chance but later was told that the authorities in Washington nixed the idea. Hopefully, some day the political climate will allow a well-controlled multi-site study of the efficacy and problems associated with an American heroin maintenance program. Until then, discussion of this potential solution must continue to remain in the realm of speculation.

Legalization

Even more open to speculation is the issue of legalization of drug use in the United States. Actually, legalization usually comes in two varieties: decriminalization and outright legalization. Proponents of decriminalization usually argue for the lowering of penalties associated with drug use. There is usually the presumption that use, or certainly sales of drugs, would probably continue to carry some legal penalties. Often, it is argued that only certain "softer drugs" such as marihuana be decriminalized. Decriminalization might take the form of converting formerly felonious behavior into misdemeanors. For instance, a person who possesses or smokes marihuana in public might be cited by a policeman in much the same way a traffic ticket is issued. Some advocates argue that while use might be decriminalized, sales might still be considered a more serious offense. Thus, decriminalization is usually a measure "halfway" between total legalization and criminalization of drug use.

The total and complete legalization of drug use has been discussed in this country for a long period of time. As you will recall from Chapter 6, for most of the history of the United States, psychoactive drugs were, by and large, totally legal. Some might argue that the country managed to survive, indeed become a great nation, despite the fact that drugs such as opium were freely available. Proposals for legalization often vary. Some persons, such as members of the Libertarian Party, argue that individuals ought to have the right to do with their bodies and minds as they wish. If they choose to abuse themselves, that is totally within their prerogative as free individuals. Others argue that psychoactive drugs should be legal but controlled in the same way that alcohol or tobacco products are now regulated. Only adults would be allowed to use the drugs, and the substances could be heavily taxed in the same way as our other legal mind-altering chemicals.

There are a number of arguments in favor of legalization of drugs. First, of course, no longer would we look upon or deal with drug users (or sellers for that matter) as criminals. The jails could be emptied of persons whose only offense was associated with the use of drugs. Adherents argue that respect for the law, particularly among the young, would increase because they would no longer engage in activities which they know are illegal. The government could control the quality of the drug, and persons would be assured of receiving a purer drug at a known dosage level. Accidental over-doses or adverse reactions to mislabelled substances would be reduced if not eliminated. The government would also receive revenue and excise taxes from the probably high sales and could use these for educational, prevention, and treatment efforts. And, finally, the amount of street crime (both property-oriented offenses and the violence associated with the street scene) would diminish markedly.

The arguments against legalization are also legion. First and foremost, the idea of legalizing these mind-altering substances flies in the face of this country's Judeo-Christian heritage, which places great emphasis on self-control. Drug use is perceived as a hedon-istic and evil activity. The idea of the government condoning (and some say through legalization encouraging) drug use is simply beyond the pale. Secondly, persons argue that we would simply be adding to the substance abuse problems we already face in America. Opponents note that there are millions of alcoholics and persons who are addicted to nicotine. These two habits cost the nation billions of dollars. Why would we want to add whole new categories of abusable substances which would lead to the creation of millions of new abusers? Even for persons who do not become addicted, there would be the problems of drug-related automobile and workplace accidents as well as lost worker productivity. Finally, there is the problem that youth, even if legally prohibited from using, would find ways to circumvent age limits as they currently do with alcohol and tobacco. In short, many opponents feel that the idea of legalization is simply so incredibly naive as not to be worth discussing.

From a sociocultural perspective, it is difficult to assess what the impact of legalization might be. One might argue that legalization of heroin would make it respectable and thus unappetizing to the "cool" street addict. Certainly legalization would disrupt drug sales and distribution networks and destroy a major source of income to street addicts. On the other hand, heroin might continue to be looked upon as "cool" (like a high priced whiskey), and the subculture would continue to flourish.

The Sociocultural Perspective

Having reviewed the major alternative to the drug problem, I would like now to develop some solutions based on the socio-cultural perspective. Throughout this book I have developed the theory that use of heroin and other street drugs is as much an indicator of an allegiance to a lifestyle as it is an "addiction" to a substance.[1] The answer to this question I believe needs to be addressed at three levels. First, the larger society needs to develop new perspectives on the drug problem. Secondly, the communities and neighborhoods where the problem of heroin addiction is most intense need to create new strategies for coping with the problem at the local level. And finally, solutions targeted specifically at the addicts themselves need to be developed.

Societally Oriented Solutions

Let us start with solutions which must be developed by the larger society. The greatest problem is that use of heroin and other street drugs is increasingly becoming more localized in the poorest and most disorganized central cities of the United States. As we saw in Chapter 1, while drug use in general is declining in the general population—even amongst our most "at risk" teenagers and young adults—the extent of serious use appears to be increasing in ghetto and lower-class inner city neighborhoods. It is clear that persons with little education, meager job skills and few alternative roles reside in these neighborhoods. It is also clear that a large measure of the blame for this situation rests with the larger society's discrimination against the country's ethnic and social class minorities. Therefore, the society needs to rectify the class and racial discrimination it finds among its own majority members.

Clearly the society must redouble its efforts to provide meaningful educational opportunities for the youth in these areas. Educational programs need to be tailored to the learning styles of these youth, fully recognizing the educational and social conditions which might hamper a youngster's ability to learn from the beginning. From a sociocultural perspective, the provision of good educational skills broadens the actor's ability to gain both a wider variety of skills and access to a greater number of legitimate roles.

The society also needs to provide more job opportunities for those who have already been caught in the web of drug abuse and despair. One cannot simply make available only the lowest-paying jobs and expect addicts to give up an exciting (and to them meaningful and potentially financially rewarding) lifestyle for the thrill of flipping burgers at a local fast-food joint. Former addicts and persons who very likely will become addicts need intensive job training and access to meaningful and rewarding jobs.

Such job training and placement programs require that addicts be assigned to counselors who have the time to invest in each addict on an individual and intimate basis. Close monitoring of the addict's behavior (including drug use) is needed. Since addiction is a chronic relapsing phenomenon, one must expect that many clients will "fail" repeatedly in such programs, but one must doggedly continue to operate and adequately fund these programmatic efforts.

The society must also provide prevention programming in all schools and other places (such as community centers, churches, playgrounds) where school dropouts, a particularly vulnerable population, are to be found. Prevention programs must be culturally relevant and must include skill-building techniques. Youth need to be taught how to develop anti-drug use values and rationales and how to resist peer pressure to use drugs. From the sociocultural perspective, youth need to learn how to avoid becoming socialized into these deviant roles.

It is also my belief that the society needs to continue to fund a wide variety of treatment programs. While I am certain that the reader has detected my skepticism about the efficacy of treatment, I nevertheless believe that treatment has an important role to play. Many persons need the emotional "crutch" of methadone or the sympathetic understanding of a therapist to help them to overcome their commitment to the street addict role.

At the present time, we have only a primitive knowledge of which treatment programs seem to work best and which individuals can be helped by these programs. We simply cannot predict what will work best, or if at all, for whom. Therefore, we need to offer a wide variety of treatment options so that individuals can choose the program which they feel will best help them.

We also need to continue to fund research programs both to develop innovative treatment approaches and to help us understand further the dynamics of which types of treatment best benefit which kinds of individuals. I also believe that much more money needs to go into social research. Large amounts of money go into the search for a "magic bullet," that elusive chemical or physiologically oriented treatment which will cure an abuser or even prevent an individual from becoming addicted. While I believe this important research needs to be continued, I also feel that we may never reach the pot of gold at the end of that rainbow. These psychoactive substances are very different from one another. Something which might block the effects of narcotics (the antagonists, for example) simply might have no effect on cocaine. A physiological solution or set of medical solutions may never be found.

Over the years I have become increasingly convinced that treatment works only for those individuals who genuinely want it to work. That is, I doubt that many individuals will give up the street addict role unless they truly want to do so. That is, they must be *motivated* to change. As I have noted above the society needs to help provide the basis for that motivation. If there are no meaningful alternatives to the street addict role, then one must not expect that individuals will change. Similarly, more research needs to be done on the dynamics of motivation. What makes persons want to change? What strategies can be employed to make the street addict role less salient and desirable to its occupants?

Finally, there is at least one other thing which the society must do—and that is, America needs to remain calm! I am convinced by Arnold Trebach's argument in *The Great Drug War* that our current drug crisis is, at least to some extent, a creation of the mass media. I believe that America has lived through at least a couple of other "drug crises" in recent history. There was, of course, the reefer madness of the thirties, the heroin crisis of the fifties, the marihuana and psychedelic problems of the sixties, the heroin epidemic of the late sixties and early seventies, and now the "crack" plague of the eighties (with the "ice" plague just around the corner). Each time, America has been told that a chemical substance was destroying our youth and thereby our country's future.

As we saw in Chapter 1, there is some encouraging evidence that in a broad sense drug use is declining in the United States. Tragically, it appears to be more and more localized in the regions least able to cope with it, namely the ghettoes, barrios, and lower-class neighborhoods of America. More and more individuals are calling for draconian measures to be employed to deal with this problem. The analogy of war is increasingly being used both in the press and by our politicians. The analogy is carried even to the extent that more active military intervention, including patrolling of American streets by soldiers, has been proposed.

As I have already said, I simply do not believe that the "drug crisis" warrants the threats to our civil liberties posed by the specter of the military assuming domestic law enforcement responsibilities. In a very real sense, this is the imposition of martial law in a situation which in my opinion is much more benign than the more usual situations in which such dramatic measures are often justified: wartime, natural disaster, or profound civil disruption. The solutions, too, which call for a suspension of traditional civil rights in criminal proceedings (such as abandonment of the need for a search warrant in a suspected drug case) constitute, in my opinion, an enormous and unprecedented threat to the civil liberties of us all. Both Watergate and Irangate more than adequately demonstrate the fact that our leaders, even at the topmost levels, cannot be trusted or invested with extraordinary authority. Does anyone believe that our civil liberties could easily be returned to us once the war on drugs was won (if indeed we were ever victorious)?

Community-oriented Solutions

As I discussed in Chapter 5, I also believe that at least part of the solution to the drug problem needs to rest in the hands of those who live in the affected communities. Primarily, these are the lower-class and inner-city areas of America. It is certainly true that these communities suffer more from the drug problem, in terms of street crime and personal tragedies, than the more middle- and upper-class suburbs. There is a rather large subculture of persons in these areas—particularly young people—who want to live life in the "fast lane." They are the potential recruits into the street addict subculture. The glamor of easy money and conspicuous consumption makes the drug dealers and users rather attractive figures in these neighborhoods of grinding poverty and despair. Somehow the values and attitudes which support the street addict lifestyle need to be changed. In other words, indigenously based movements need to be developed whereby the street addict lifestyle is not seen as glamorous or even desirable. This will be a slow and tortured process. As sociologists have pointed out for decades, values change slowly.

However, I believe we see the beginnings of a shift in value structures in many of these communities. Jesse Jackson made it a centerpiece of his presidential campaign. Community groups around the country are beginning to ban "crack" dealers from their neighborhoods and report the presence of "crack houses" to the police. Muslims and other groups are trying to "take back" some of their neighborhoods. Other groups in public housing are mounting citizen patrols and developing community campaigns against the use of drugs.

I believe these efforts need to be supported both financially and with the moral authority and other resources of the government. These groups require money in order to launch successful efforts against drug use. They also need the presence and protection of the police. Every effort must be made to protect them from retaliation by street sellers and delinquent gangs which might object to the community organizations limiting their ability to sell and use drugs in these areas.

Addict-oriented Solutions

The theme of this book has been that street addicts are generally what I would refer to as a "rational actors." To a large extent, they "choose" to become street addicts. However, remember that this "choice" is conditioned by the socioeconomic circumstances in which the vast majority of addicts find themselves. The street addict role is one of only a few relatively rewarding roles open to most persons who become street addicts. Therefore, we need not "blame the victims" for choosing one of the very limited number of available roles.

Nevertheless, we must recognize that the addict can make rational choices. If the street addict role becomes too onerous or burdensome, or if other roles can be made more attractive, most persons will abandon the street addict role. This is essentially what Biernacki's fine analysis of the pathways from addiction demonstrates. The street addict role simply becomes incompatible with other roles the addict wants to play. The society has by and large attempted to make the street addict role an "expensive" one by levying heavy legal and social penalties on it. I believe we could continue in that direction by increasing the penalties ever higher. Such efforts might reduce the number of street addicts. But this would be accomplished at an unacceptably great legal, economic, and moral cost to America.

There are some things happening in the community which I believe are making the role more undesirable. As noted, there are the efforts of community groups to define the addict lifestyle as evil and stupid. Young persons, not already swept up in the drug life, may continue to insulate themselves from the lifestyle. Even more importantly, there is AIDS. Some areas, such as New York City and northern New Jersey, report seropositivity rates of 60 percent or higher among intravenous drug users. The result has been predictable; addicts are flocking to treatment centers in an attempt to escape addiction and the threat of AIDS. Indeed, treatment program waiting lists of up to one year's duration are reported in these high seropositivity areas. Most persons, when faced with a genuine chance of dying because of their behavior, will attempt to change that behavior. It may be that AIDS will provide one source of motivation for change.

Behaviorists tell us that persons respond to positive as well as negative rewards. Thus, the motivation for change can also come about if persons feel they have a meaningful alternative to their present lifestyles. Again, the society needs to provide roles which can genuinely replace that of the street addict. More creative thinking needs to be done in developing such roles. And I believe that addicts need to be involved in that endeavor.

Let me give you a few examples of what I am talking about. The street addict value structure highly evaluates manipulative behavior and "smooth talking." Employment counselors should assess the importance of these values when trying to place their clients. I remember a client once telling me that the "square" job he most enjoyed in his life was as a shoe salesman. He felt that convincing buyers to purchase shoes was most like the "conning" he had to do as an addict. That job gave him a sense of accomplishment and he truly enjoyed it.

Similarly, addicts need to be taught the ways of the middle class. Few know even how to go about seeking out a job. They do not know how to find potential employment (except at the most menial level) and lack the social skills of the middle class in appropriate job interview demeanor, etc. In addition to providing addicts with culturally appropriate job skills, they need also to be provided with job seeking and on-the-job behavior skills. They need to be taught the importance of punctuality and acceptance of responsibility on the job. They also need to be taught how to interact with fellow employees. From the sociocultural perspective they need to be provided with new roles and educated, through adult socialization, into these new roles.

Ultimately, street addicts need to learn in treatment, in interactions with others, and with societal agents that true and lasting change in both their behavior and self concepts can occur only if they take responsibility for their own behavior. I suppose one of the reasons I am skeptical of the disease models is because ultimate responsibility for the behavior is placed outside of the individual. I believe street addicts must both be empowered and empower themselves for active constructive change in their life circumstances. However, as I have said before, such expectation for change is difficult without adequate educational, societal, and economic resources being provided to facilitate that change.

Conclusion

We have finally come to the end of the journey I promised you in the first chapter. I hope that I have convinced you that addiction to narcotics (and to many other "street drugs," as well) needs to be looked at in the larger sociocultural context in which it occurs. Rather than looking at addicts as pitiable, "sick" individuals, it might be profitable to view them as persons who are attempting to carve meaningful existential identities in economically and socially devastating conditions. The causes of the "drug problem" in this country are extremely complex. Similarly, the "solution" is not simple. Indeed, the "cure" for America's drug illness must be developed at all levels: the society, the community, and the individual.

Notes

Chapter 1

1. The concept of physical addiction has come under attack by Peele (1985).

Chapter 2

1. Actually, in this chapter, I discuss the contributions of both symbolic interactionists and role theorists whose perspective, while being somewhat different, nevertheless complement each other's. While there are differences between role theory and symbolic interactionism, the theory which I develop attempts to integrate the insights of both perspectives, and it is in this spirit that I discuss them as though they constituted a single body of theoretical work.

2. Heiss (1981) argues that the self-concept is not the same as the self. He sees the self as process and the self-concept as the organized set of self-attitudes. It would seem that in our scheme, the self-concept would be what Hewitt (1984) calls the "object."

3. This is especially true for the present work since the sociocultural approach discussed later emphasizes the orientation of the actor and his or her expectations for self.

4. Heiss suggests that these two positions are not as extreme or different as many would think. (Heiss, 1981: 96–101).

5. Indeed, I would argue this is why one of the first questions one is asked by strangers in many situations is, "What do you do for a living?" In American society, it is a good way to "map" individuals and thus be able to predict both their behavior and many of their attitudes.

6. For further discussion of this issue, see Turner (1962).

7. One exception is Cardwell (1971), who defines it as "the totality of man's symbolic heritage" (Cardwell, 1971: 54).

8. See, for instance, Cohen's (1955) discussion of the subculture of delinquent boys.

9. For a social learning theory explanation of socialization, see Heiss (1981).

10. The self is central to many theoretical explanations of heroin addiction. For a review of these uses, see Stephens (1982).

11. Labelling theory also pays great attention to how behavior comes to be labelled as deviant. See, for example, Becker's (1963) discussion of moral entrepreneurs.

12. Societally structured constraints on access to roles is one of the principal underlying concepts of control theory (Hirschi, 1969).

Chapter 3

1. This chapter is a revised and expanded version of a paper first published in the *Journal of Drug Issues* (Stephens, 1985).

2. Of course, many of my anthropologically trained colleagues might not agree that development of hypothesis-based theories is appropriate to ethnography. See, for instance, Agar's (1980) discussion, particularly pages 69–81 and 171–173.

3. There have been a number of attempts to build typologies of heroin addicts. (See, for instance, Bates and Crowther [1974] and Levine and Stephens [1973].) One of the most recent is the excellent work by David Nurco and his associates (Nurco, et al., 1981). Their typology of narcotics users is empirically derived and is based on the users' investment in drug-taking as a central life interest and the degree to which it dominates their other life activities. I conceive of the types described in the works cited above as showing different degrees of commitment to the street addict role.

4. This term is used to denote, in a non-derogatory way, the members of the drug subculture and in fact often is used to refer to themselves.

5. Junkies are also included in the class of drug users known as multiple-drug users. That is, most narcotics addicts use a range of other psychoactive substances, including cocaine, marihuana, alcohol, and other drugs. However, almost all are emotionally committed to the regular use of heroin (and other street narcotics and cocaine) as a fundamental "hallmark" of their street addict status.

6. For a discussion of ideal types, see Martindale (1960), especially pages 381–383.

7. In order to keep the focus on the theoretical framework, only enough empirical literature will be cited to confirm the veridicality of the propositions and hypotheses. Fuller support for the general theoretical framework will be provided in Chapter 4.

8. One note of caution should be offered as regards the theory being proposed here. The theory is based on what we currently know (or at least think we know) about the great majority of urban heroin addicts (who anchor one end of the heroin use continuum). Much of this knowledge is based on work published in the 1960s and 1970s although the theory appears to be supported by more recent studies including those by Rosenbaum (1981), Johnson, et al. (1985), and Biernacki (1986). Hanson, et al. (1985) also provide analyses which support some, but not all, of the theory. The ways in which their work question the theory will be more fully discussed later in this chapter.

There remains the possibility that significant, yet undetected, changes could have occurred in the street scene. One such instance occurred several years ago when there was widespread fear of a middle-class heroin user epidemic. These rather affluent, young heroin users were described in an article which appeared in *Rolling Stone* magazine. While one thrust of the article seemed to be that this was a different breed of heroin user, I was as struck by the similarities to the typical addict as I was by the supposed differences. The article described behaviors such as extensive lying and stealing in which the new users had presumably not previously engaged. In quoting a dealer, these young users were described thusly: "For a lot of young people, it's the image. You're the cool guy, the guy who's on smack. You're part of a minority. A little bit more adventurous, dangerous, antisocial" (Haden-Guest, 1983: 26). As we shall see, this description is remarkably like the street addict we will be examining in great detail. Thus, we may actually be observing the process of these young users becoming more typical street addicts. Or it is possible that such individuals always existed but were undetected by researchers. Having said all of this, the caveat about changes in the street scene over time still has to be made.

9. Our original discussion of role did not clearly differentiate between behavioral expectations and actual behavior. The present discussion is consistent with my definition of role as behavioral expectation.

10. This trait seems to be supported by the high scores addicts often obtain on sensation-seeking scales. For a review of the relevant studies see Platt (1986).

11. This trait is also supported by the psychological literature. According to Platt (1986), the addict has a significantly less extended future time perspective.

12. This comment about nonviolence among addicts may no longer be valid (McBride, 1981).

13. Undoubtedly, the street addict role is a product of many forces. It results from: the illegality of heroin use, the functional needs of the addict to obtain heroin and the money needed to purchase heroin, and the environmental value structure in which much heroin use is found. The origins and development of the street addict role will be explored in greater detail in Chapter 6 of this book.

14. As I have noted, role cannot be operationalized in terms of behavior but rather as behavioral expectations. Thus, it is not appropriate to call this attempt a true operationalization of role. Rather, it is an operationalization of role behaviors. A candid confession—when this study was conducted in the early seventies, I had not clearly differentiated between the two.

15. To be perfectly fair, it should be pointed out that some studies have found that addicts have more traditional value structures. These studies, conducted with paper and pencil type instruments, are reviewed by Platt (1986). Part of the explanation may be that these tests were administered in treatment settings where perhaps the worldview of the addict may have changed. Other than this possible explanation, I can only say that my reading of the sociocultural literature would not support the viewpoint that addicts have conventional value structures.

16. As with most interactionist theory, the direction of causality is not one way; there are feedback mechanisms imbedded in the model. Hence, as one becomes more involved in the life, one uses more heroin which in turn leads to even greater socialization (or acculturation) into the street addict role.

17. For a review of these theories, see Stephens (1982) and selected theories as presented in Lettieri, et al., (1980).

18. Relapse is such an important recurring phenomenon among addicts that Lindesmith (1968: 55) used it, along with craving, as one of the defining characteristics of addiction (as contrasted to the more fundamentally physiological process of habituation).

19. Remember that once an individual has undergone withdrawal and has remained "clean" for a relatively short period of time, there is no reason to suspect that there is a physiological necessity to re-use, as is the case when the person is physically addicted.

20. In one study controlled users were defined as persons "who were required to be over 18 and to have used opiates at least 10 times per year for more than 2 years and at least 2 times during the 6 months preceding the interview. They must not have had more than one "spree"—an instance of from 4 to 15 consecutive days of opiate use—in any of these years. With the exception of tobacco they must have been using all drugs, licit and illicit, in a controlled way

and must not have been in a drug-free or methadone maintenance program, in jail or in any other confining institution during their years of controlled use" (Zinberg, 1979: 306).

Chapter 4

1. For a more in-depth review of some of the literature on the precursors of addiction—especially the psychologically based studies—see Nurco (1982).

2. For a further exploration of the drift hypothesis as applied to delinquency, see Matza (1964).

3. Some older studies (Waldorf, 1973; Hendler and Stephens, 1977) have shown that the route of first use is usually "snorting." "Snorting" was often used because both the potentially dangerous impact of the heroin is lessened and many people fear the hypodermic needle. More recent studies indicate that neophytes seem now to prefer the intravenous route. (See, for instance, Hanson, et al. [1985] and Hser, Anglin, and McGlothlin, [1987].)

4. Becker has pointed out the powerful influence of the group in shaping the user's perception of the appreciation for drug effects (Becker, 1963).

5. Researchers (Alksne, Lieberman, and Brill, 1967; O'Donnell, 1968 and Rosenbaum, 1981) point to the symbolic importance of the intravenous route. It is at the point when the user turns to the regular use of the needle that commitment to the street addict role begins in earnest.

6. As I noted in Chapter 2, Lindesmith (1968) argues that recognition by the user that the distress of withdrawal is due to the absence of narcotics in the body leads to the formation of the self-concept as an addict. Lindesmith also argues that the motivation for use changes from one of getting high to one of "staying straight" (that is, avoiding withdrawal). There is no doubt in my mind that recognition of one's physical addiction is a crucial step in confirming the self-concept as an addict. This was a brilliant social-psychological insight by Lindesmith. However, I feel that addicts are nevertheless still motivated to get "high" even after they become physically addicted (see the cogent argument by McAuliffe and Gordon [1974]). Addicts first take care of their habit (by avoiding withdrawal), but if drugs are left over, they will take them in an attempt to get "high."

7. Indeed, Fraser and Hawkins (1984) show that this process seems to apply more to opiate abusers than to abusers of non-opiates. Opiate abusers' networks are less involved in conventional activities and significantly more involved in street crime. Correspondingly, opiate abusers have fewer contacts with members from social clubs, church, athletic groups, with family members and friends, and with work or school groups.

8. These figures include the total retail value of the drugs, whether they were purchased or acquired in some other way. Heroin users who used heroin zero, one, or two days per week on average were defined as irregular users. Regular users consumed heroin four or five days per week. Those who used heroin more frequently are daily users.

9. While these types of criminal addicts can be identified, it is important to note that any individual addict is likely to commit a wide variety of crimes. As this typology indicates, addicts do engage in some degree of specialization. But as data provided by Johnson, et al. (1985) illustrate, large percentages of addicts engage in robbery, burglary, shoplifting, other larcenies, and confidence games. In fact, the type of activity—whether legal, semi-legal or illegal—the addict will choose to generate income on any particular day is almost a chance decision. That is, few criminal activities are carefully planned; most are what Goldstein (1981: 69) calls "opportunistic."

10. Two points need to be made about violence among addicts. First, it appears that the prevalence of violent activity is indeed increasing among addicts (Stephens and Ellis, 1975; McBride, 1981). Maddux and Desmond (1981) found that 44 percent of their sample had been arrested for a violent crime and about a quarter had been a victim of gunshot or knife wounds. In fact, homicide was the leading cause of death among their addict sample (Maddux and Desmond, 1981). Whether increases in violent activity are due to the fact (as one old-time addict told me) that "lower quality people" are becoming addicts or, as is more likely, to other factors remains to be seen.

Secondly, as Goldstein (1985) has pointed out, much violence in the street addict world is systemic, that is violence intrinsic to the system of drug distribution and use. This includes: punishment of dealers by distributors for shortchanging, "wars" between sellers for territory, and robbery of dealers.

11. Recall that daily use was defined as use of six or seven days per week, regular use was three to five days, and irregular use was zero to two days.

12. Obviously excluded in this definition of crime are possession and use offenses; in this sense, all narcotics users are *ipso facto* criminals.

13. Caplovitz's definition of the term addicted appears to be very general. Whether these individuals were truly physiologically addicted is not very clear to me.

14. Possibly this finding further confirms the idea that they were less committed to the street addict role than the unemployed addicts. Also their current work roles may not have been congruent with the street addict role.

15. Ellis and Stephens (1976) show that dysfunctional behavior, at least as measured by frequency of arrests, increases in the year before admission to a treatment program.

Chapter 5

1. Many of these criticisms are discussed in Stephens (1987).

2. I must admit that with the relatively recent emergence of the AIDS epidemic among intravenous drug users, my argument about the addict's rationality appears strained. It is difficult to believe that any rational human being would run the great risk of contracting AIDS that intravenous drug users do. However, it appears from some preliminary literature that many addicts are beginning to revise their needle-sharing behavior and are engaging in needle-cleaning techniques. Additionally, many are seeking treatment. This phenomenon has created long waiting lists of clients for East Coast treatment clinics.

3. As we discussed in Chapter 1, the long term effects of heroin may not be as harmful as those of tobacco.

Chapter 6

1. For a somewhat more complete discussion, see Stephens (1987).

2. I am indebted to Michael Agar for this insight.

3. Much more detailed descriptions and analyses of this street-corner world are found in Liebow (1967) and Anderson (1978).

4. While the studies I have reviewed focus primarily on the black ghetto, it is clear that many lower-class whites share some of the same values. An interesting analysis is presented by MacLeod (1987), who

studied two adolescent peer groups in a lower-income predominantly white neighborhood. One was white and shared many of the values enumerated by Hannerz, while the black group was much more oriented to middle-class American values, particularly the work and success ethics.

Chapter 7

1. I employ the term "blockade" with much misgiving. In fact, only the narcotic antagonists such as cyclazocine, Nalline, and naloxone truly block the effects of the narcotic agonists. However, a high enough dose of methadone will, through the process of cross-tolerance, insure that the addict will not ordinarily get high with a pharmacologically smaller dose of heroin or any other narcotic.

2. This insight was first provided by Michael Agar.

3. Whenever I deal with this issue I am reminded of a methadone maintenance client with whom I worked for several years. He was a fine young man who had established a typical middle-class lifestyle. Yet, he was never quite able to completely get himself off of methadone. He had been able to reduce his dosage to 5 mg per day, an almost pharmacologically inert amount. Yet, whenever he tried to take that final step to complete abstinence, he always failed. His behavior would become erratic and he would be forced to return to that small dose. Quite frankly, I always wondered if he might truly be a case of a person suffering from a metabolic deficiency.

4. One of the best discussions of the transformation of a therapeutic community into an organization which abused its members is provided by Robert Weppner in an extremely well-written and insightful book entitled *The Untherapeutic Community* (1983).

5. While many individuals are severely critical of allegiance to such a lifestyle, I must admit that while the lifestyle does not appeal to me, it appears to be much better for these individuals than their previous lives as street addicts. They have become happy and productive citizens who feel that they are making meaningful contributions to society both through their occupations (many work in t.c. industries or even in the community) and through their commitment to help others with drug problems.

6. It is interesting to note that we often talk about a medication or treatment "failing." Indeed, there have been hundreds of studies of the

effectiveness of different treatment modalities. Typically, these studies do not characterize the clients as having failed, but rather the programs as having not succeeded in changing client behavior.

Chapter 8

1. I have addressed the problem of what is to be done in some detail elsewhere. However, much of that discussion did not flow directly from the sociocultural perspective. Accordingly, I will develop a different strategy in this chapter which compliments my other work.

References

Agar, Michael. 1971. "Folklore of the Heroin Addict: Two Examples." *Journal of American Folklore* 33:175-85.

_____. 1973. *Ripping and Running.* New York: Seminar Press.

_____. 1980. *The Professional Stranger: An Informal Introduction to Ethnography.* New York: Academic Press.

Alksne, H., L. Lieberman and L. Brill. 1967. "A Conceptual Model of the Life Cycle of Addiction." *International Journal of the Addictions* 2(2):221-241.

Anderson, Elijah. 1978. *A Place on the Corner.* Chicago: University of Chicago Press.

Anglin, M. Douglas. 1987. "Sex Difference in Addict Careers. 2 Becoming Addicted." *American Journal of Drug and Alcohol Abuse* 13(1,2):59-71.

Ashery, Rebecca. 1983. *Psychotherapy For Methadone Maintained Opiate Addicts: A Report of Two Studies.* Washington, DC: National Institute on Drug Abuse.

Ball, John C., John W. Shaffer, and David N. Nurco. 1983. *The Day-To-Day Criminality of Heroin Addicts in Baltimore—A Study in the Continuity of Offence Rates.* Drug and Alcohol Dependence, 12:119-142.

_____. and R. W. Snarr. 1969. "A Test of the Maturation Hypothesis With Respect to Opiate Addiction." *Bulletin on Narcotics* 21:9-13.

Bates, William and Betty Crowther. 1974. *Towards A Typology of Opiate Users.* Cambridge, Mass.: Schenkman.

Becker, Howard. 1963. *Outsiders.* New York: Free Press.

Biddle, Bruce J. 1979. *Role Theory.* New York: Acedemic Press.

Biernacki, Patrick. 1986. *Pathways From Heroin Addiction: Recovery Without Treatment.* Philadelphia, Pa.: Temple University Press.

Blumer, Herbert. 1969. *Symbolic Interactionism: Perspective and Method.* Englewood Cliffs, N.J.: Prentice-Hall.

Brill, Leon. 1972. *The De-Addiction Process: Studies in the De-Addiction of Confirmed Heroin Addicts.* Springfield, Ill.: Charles C. Thomas.

_____ and L. Lieberman. 1969. *Authority and Addiction.* Boston, Mass.: Little, Brown.

_____, George Nash, and John Langrod. 1972. "The Dynamics of De-Addiction: A Pilot Study," in Leon Brill and Louis Lieberman (eds.) *Major Modalities in the Treatment of Drug Abuse.* New York: Behavioral.

Brim, Orville G., Jr. 1966. "Socialization Through the Life Cycle," in Orville Brim, Jr., and Stanton Wheeler (eds.) *Socialization After Childhood.* New York: Wiley.

Brown, B. S., S. K. Guavey, M. B. Mayers, and S. D. Stark. 1971. "In Their Own Words: Addicts' Reasons for Initiating and Withdrawing from Heroin." *International Journal of the Addictions* 6:635–645.

Brown, C. 1965. *Manchild in the Promised Land.* New York: New American Library.

Burroughs, W. 1953. *Junkie.* New York: Ace Books.

Capel, W. C., B. M. Goldsmith, K. J. Waddel, et al. 1972. "The Aging Narcotic Addict: An Increasing Problem for the Next Two Decades." *Journal of Gerontology* 27:102–106.

_____ and G. T. Stewart. 1971. "The Management of Drug Abuse in Aging Populations: New Orleans Findings." *Journal of Drug Issues* 1:114–121.

Caplovitz, David. 1976. *The Working Addict.* White Plains, N.Y.: Sharpe.

Cardwell, J. D. 1971. *Social Psychology: A Symbolic Interactionalist Perspective.* Philadelphia: F. A. Davis.

Cohen, Albert K. 1955. *Delinquent Boys.* Glencoe, Ill.: Free Press.

Courtwright, David T. 1982. *Dark Paradise.* Cambridge, Mass.: Harvard University Press.

Cox, Terrance, M. R. Jacobs, A. E. Leblanc, and J. A. Marshman. 1983. *Drugs and Drug Abuse: A Reference Text.* Toronto, Canada: Addiction Research Foundation.

Craig, S. R. and B. S. Brown. 1975. "Comparison of Youthful Heroin Users and Non-Users From One Urban Community." *International Journal of the Addictions* 10:53–64.

Crawford, Gail, Melvin C. Washington, and Edward C. Senay. 1980. "Early Life Style Differences Among Black Male Heroin Addicts and Their Non-Addicted Friends." *American Journal of Drug and Alcohol Abuse* 7(2):193–210.

_____, Melvin C. Washington, and Edward C. Senay. 1983. "Careers With Heroin." *International Journal of the Addictions* 18(5):701–715.

Delgaty, Robert. 1976. "Heroin Use in Niagara Falls, Ontario." *Addictive Diseases* 2:403–419.

Dembo, Richard, W. Burgos, D. V. Babst, J. Schmeidler, and L. LaGrand. 1978. "Neighborhood Relationships and Drug Involvement Among Inner City Junior High School Youths: Implications for Drug Education and Prevention Programming." *Journal of Drug Education* 8:231–252.

_____, Dana Farrow, James Schmeidler, and William Burgos. 1979. "Testing a Causal Model of Environmental Influences on the Early Drug Involvement of Inner City Junior High School Youths." *American Journal of Drug and Alcohol Abuse* 6(3):313–336.

Dole, Vincent and Marie E. Nyswander. 1980. "Methadone Maintenance: A Theoretical Perspective," in D. J. Lettieri, M. Sayers, and H. Wallenstein Pearson (eds.) *Theories on Drug Abuse.* Washington DC: National Institute on Drug Abuse.

Duster, Troy. 1970. *The Legalization of Morality: Laws, Drugs and Moral Judgment.* New York: Free Press.

Eldred, C. A. and M. N. Washington. 1975. "Female Heroin Addicts in a City Treatment Program: The Forgotten Minority." *Psychiatry.* 38(1):75–85.

_____. 1976. "Interpersonal Relationships in Heroin Use by Men and Women and Their Role in Treatment Outcome." *International Journal of the Addictions.* (ICI): 117–130.

Elliott, D., D. Huizinga, and S. Ageton. 1985. *Explaining Delinquency and Drug Use.* Beverly Hills, Calif.: Sage.

Ellis, Rosalind and Richard C. Stephens. 1976. "The Arrest History of Narcotic Addicts Prior to Admission: A Methodological Note." *Drug Forum* 5(3):211–224.

Feldman, Harvey. 1968. "Ideological Supports to Becoming and Remaining a Heroin Addict." *Journal of Health and Social Behavior* 9(2): 131–139.

Feucht, Thomas, Richard C. Stephens, and Shadi W. Roman. 1990 (forthcoming). "The Sexual Behavior of Intravenous Drug Users: Assessing the Risk of Sexual Transmission of HIV." *Journal of Drug Issues*.

Fiddle, Seymour. 1967. *Portrait From a Shooting Gallery*. New York: Harper and Row.

———. 1969. "Some Speculations on Risk Discounting Among Youth Ghetto Heroin Users." Paper presented at the National Leadership Conference of the American Social Health Association.

File, K. N. 1976. "Sex Roles and Street Roles." *International Journal of the Addictions* 11(2):263–268.

Finestone, H. 1964. "Cats, Kicks and Color," in Howard Becker (ed.) *The Otherside*. New York: Free Press.

Fingarette, Herbert. 1988. *Heavy Drinking*. Los Angeles, Calif.: University of California Press.

Fort, J. 1969. *The Pleasure Seekers*. New York: Bobbs-Merrill.

Fraser, Mark and J. David Hawkins. 1984. "The Social Networks of Opioid Abusers." *International Journal of the Addictions* 19(8): 903–917.

Gandossy, R. P., J. R. Williams, J. Cohen, et al. 1980. *Drugs and Crime: A Survey and Analysis of the Literature*. Washington, DC: U.S. Government Printing Office.

Gans, Herbert J. 1962. *Villagers*. New York: Free Press.

Gay, George R., E. Senay, and J. A. Newmeyer. 1973. "The Pseudo-Junkie: Evolution of the Heroin Lifestyle in the Non-Addicted Individual." *Drug Forum* 2:279–290.

Gendreau, P. and L. P. Gendreau. 1970. "The 'Addiction-Prone' Personality: A Study of Canadian Heroin Addicts." *Canadian Journal of Behavioral Science* 2:18–25.

———. 1971. "Research Design and Narcotic Addiction Proneness." *Canadian Psychiatric Association Journal* 16:265–267.

_____. 1973. "A Theoretical Note on Personality Characteristics of Heroin Addicts." *Journal of Abnormal Psychology* 82:139-140.

Gerth, Hans and C. Wright Mills. 1953. *Character and Social Structure.* New York: Harcourt, Brace and World.

Gibbons, L. G., B. S. Brown, M. H. Greene, and R. L. DuPont. 1981. "Initiation Into Heroin Use." *International Journal of the Addictions* 16:935-939.

Glaser, Daniel. 1956. "Criminality Theories and Behavioral Images." *American Journal of Sociology* 29:669-679.

_____, Bernard Lander, and William Abbott. 1971. "Opiate Addicted and Non-Addicted Siblings in a Slum Area." *Social Problems.* 18 (Spring): 510-521.

Goffman, Irvin L. 1959. *The Presentation of Self in Everyday Life.* New York: Anchor Books.

Goldstein, Paul J. 1981. "Getting Over: Economic Alternatives to Predatory Crime Among Street Drug Users," in James A. Inciardi (ed.) *The Drugs/Crime Connection.* Beverly Hills, Calif.: Sage.

_____. 1985. "The Drugs/Violence Nexus: A Tripartite Conceptual Framework." *Journal of Drug Issues* 15:493-506.

_____ and N. S. Duchaine. 1979. "Daily Criminal Activities of Street Drug Users." Presented at the Meetings of the American Society of Criminology, Philadelphia.

Goode, William J. 1960. "A Theory of Role Strain." *American Sociological Review* 25:483-496.

Gould, Leroy C., Andrew L. Walker, Lansing E. Crane, and Charles W. Lidz. 1974. *Connections: Notes from the Heroin World.* New Haven, Conn.: Yale University Press.

Gross, Neal, Ward S. Mason, and Alexander W. McEachern. 1958. *Explorations in Role Analysis.* New York: Wiley.

Gusfield, Joseph. 1963. *Symbolic Crusade.* Champaign: University of Illinois Press.

Haden-Guest, Anthony. 1983. "Rich Kids on Smack: The Young, The Rich, and Heroin." *Rolling Stone,* 399 (July 7, 1983).

Haertzer, C. A., T. R. Kocher, and K. Miyasato. 1983. "Reinforcements from the First Drug Can Predict Later Drug Habits and/or Addiction: Results with Coffee, Cigarettes. Alcohol, Barbiturates, Minor and Major Tranquilizers, Stimulants, Marijuana, Hallucinogens, Heroin and Opiates." *Drug and Alcohol Dependence* 11:147–165.

Hannerz, U. 1969. *Soulside: Inquiries into Ghetto Culture and Community.* New York: Lifestyle Press.

Hanson, Bill, G. Beschner, J. M. Walters, and E. Bovelle. 1985. *Life With Heroin.* Lexington, Mass.: Lexington Books.

Heiss, Jerold. 1981. "Social Roles," in Morris Rosenberg and Ralph H. Turner (eds.) *Social Psychology: Sociological Perspectives.* New York: Basic Books.

Helmer, John. 1975. *Drugs and Minority Oppression.* New York: Seabury Press.

Hendler, H. and Richard C. Stephens. 1977. "The Addict Odyssey: From Experimentation to Addiction." *International Journal of the Addictions* 12(1):25–42.

Hewitt, John. 1984. *Self and Society.* 3rd ed. Boston, Mass.: Allyn and Bacon.

Hirschi, Travis. 1969. *The Causes of Delinquency.* Los Angeles: University of California Press.

Hofmann, Frederick G. 1975. *A Handbook on Drug and Alcohol Abuse: The Biomedical Aspects.* New York: Oxford University Press.

Hser, Yih-Ing, M. Douglas Anglin and William McGlothin. 1987. "Sex Differences in Addict Careers" I. "Initiation of Use." *American Journal of Drug and Alcohol Abuse* 13(1,2):33–58.

Hughes, E. C. 1945. "Dilemmas and Contradictions of Status." *American Journal of Sociology* 50:353–359.

Hughes, Patrick H. 1977. *Behind the Wall of Respect.* Chicago, Ill.: University of Chicago Press.

Inciardi, James A. 1977. *Methadone Diversion: Experience and Issues.* Washington, D.C.: National Institute on Drug Abuse.

_____. 1981. *The Drugs/Crime Connection.* Beverly Hills, Calif.: Sage.

———. 1986. *The War on Drugs: Heroin, Cocaine and Public Policy.* Palo Alto, Calif.: Mayfield.

——— and C. D. Chambers. 1972. "Criminal Involvement of Narcotic Addicts." *Journal of Drugs Issues* 2:57–64.

Jessor, Richard and S. L. Jessor. 1977. *Problem Behavior and Psychosocial Development: A Longitudinal Study of Youth.* New York: Academic Press.

Johnson, Bruce D., Paul J. Goldstein, Edward Preble, James Schmeidler, Douglas S. Lipton, Barry Spunt, and Thomas Miller. 1985. *Taking Care of Business: The Economics of Crime by Heroin Abusers.* Lexington, Mass.: Lexington Books.

Kandel, D. 1974. "Interpersonal Influences on Adolescent Illegal Drug Use," in E. Josephson and E. Carroll (eds.) *Drug Use Epidemiological and Sociological Approaches.* New York: Wiley.

Kaplan, John. 1983. *The Hardest Drug.* Chicago, Ill.: University of Chicago Press.

Lang, Alan R. 1983. "Addictive Personality: A Viable Construct?" in P. K. Levison, D. R. Gerstein, and D. R. Maloff (eds.) *Commonalities in Substance Abuse and Habitual Behavior.* Lexington, Mass.: D.C. Heath.

Leavitt, Fred. 1982. *Drugs and Behavior* 2nd ed. New York: Wiley.

Lemert, Edwin. 1951. *Social Pathology.* New York: McGraw-Hill.

Lettieri, Dan J., M. Sayers, and H. W. Pearson. 1980. *Theories on Drug Abuse.* NIDA Research Monograph 30. Washington, DC: National Institute on Drug Abuse.

Leukefeld, Carl G. and Frank M. Tims. 1988. *Compulsory Treatment of Drug Abuse: Research and Clinical Practice.* Rockville, Md.: National Insitute on Drug Abuse.

Levine, Stephen and Richard C. Stephens. 1972. "Games Addicts Play." *Psychiatric Quarterly* 45:1–11.

———. 1973. "Types of Narcotic Addicts," in Richard E. Hardy and John G. Cull (eds.) *Drug Addiction and Rehabilitation Approaches.* Springfield, Ill.: Charles C. Thomas.

Lewis, Oscar. 1966. *La Vida: A Puerto Rican Family in the Culture of Poverty—San Juan and New York*. New York: Random House.

Liebow, Elliot. 1967. *Tally's Corner: A Study of Negro Street Corner Men*. Boston, Mass.: Little Brown.

Lindesmith, Alfred R. 1968. *Addiction and Opiates*. Chicago, Ill.: Aldine.

Linton, Ralph. 1936. *The Study of Man*. New York: Appleton-Century.

Liska, Ken. 1986. *Drugs and the Human Body: With Implications for Society*. 2nd ed. New York: MacMillan.

Lofland, John. 1969. *Deviance and Identity*. Englewood Cliffs, N.J.: Prentice Hall.

MacCleod, Jay. 1987. *Ain't No Making It: Leveled Aspirations in a Low-Income Neighborhood*. Boulder, Colo.: Western Press.

Maddux, James F. and David P. Desmond. 1981. *Careers of Opioid Users*. New York: Praeger.

_____. 1984. "Heroin Addicts and Non-Addicted Brothers." *American Journal of Drug and Alcohol Abuse* 10(2):237–248.

Maines, David R. 1977. "Social Organization and Social Structure in Symbolic Interactionist Thought," in Alex Inkeles, James Coleman, and Neil Smelser (eds.) *Annual Review of Sociology*. Palo Alto, Calif.: Annual Reviews Inc.

Martindale, Don. 1960. *The Nature and Types of Sociological Theory*. Boston: Houghton Mifflin.

Matza, David. 1964. *Delinquency and Drift*. New York: Wiley.

_____. 1969. *Becoming Deviant*. Englewood Cliffs, N.J.: Prentice-Hall.

McAuliffe, William E. 1975. "Beyond Secondary Deviance: Negative Labelling and Its Effects on the Heroin Addict." in Grove, Walter R. *The Labelling of Deviance*. New York: Wiley.

_____. 1975. "A Second Look at First Effects: The Subjective Effects of Opiates on Nonaddicts." *Journal of Drug Issues*. 5(4).

_____. and J. A. Gordon. 1974. "A Test of Lindesmith's Theory of Addiction: The Frequency of Euphoria Among Long-Term Addicts," in R. H. Coombs, L. J. Fry, and P. G. Lewis (eds.) *Socialization in Drug Abuse*. Cambridge, Mass.: Schenkman.

McBride, Duane C. 1981. "Drugs and Violence," in James Inciardi (ed.) *The Drugs/Crime Connection*. Beverly Hills, Calif.: Sage.

McCall, George J. and J. L. Simmons. 1978. *Identities and Interactions*. New York: Free Press.

McKay, Virginia. 1980. *Non-Addictive Heroin Use*. M.A. Thesis, University of Houston.

Mead, George Herbert. 1934. *Mind, Self, and Society*. Chicago, Ill.: University of Chicago Press.

Meltzer, B. M., J. W. Petras, and L. T. Reynolds. 1975. *Symbolic Interactionism: Genesis, Varieties and Criticisms*. Boston: Portledt and K. Paul.

Merton, R. K. 1957. "Social Structure and Anomie," in R. K. Merton (ed.) *Social Theory and Social Structure*. Glencoe, Ill.: Free Press.

Miller, Walter B. 1958. "Lower Class Culture as a Generating Milieu of Gang Delinquency." *Journal of Social Issues* 14(3):5–19.

Morgan, H. Wayne. 1981. *Drugs in America*. Syracuse, N.Y.: Syracuse University Press.

Musto, David F. 1973. *The American Disease*. New Haven, Conn.: Yale University Press.

National Institute of Justice. 1989. *Drug Use Forecasting (DUF), Fourth Quarter 1988*. Washington, D.C.: U.S. Department of Justice.

Nurco, David N. 1982. *Precursors of Addiction. NIDA Research Monograph 41*. Washington, D.C.: U.S. Government Printing Office.

———, John C. Ball, John W. Shaffer, and Thomas Hanlon. 1985. "The Criminality of Narcotic Addicts." *Journal of Nervous Mental Diseases* 173:94–102.

———, Ira H. Cisin, and Mitchell B. Balter. 1981a. "Addict Careers" I. "A New Typology." *The International Journal of the Addictions* 16:1305–1325.

———, Ira H. Cisin, and Mitchell B. Balter. 1981b. "Addict Careers" II. "The First Ten Years." *The International Journal of the Addictions* 16(8):1327–1356.

_____, Ira H. Cisin, and Mitchell B. Balter. 1981c. "Addict Careers" III. "Trends Across Time." *The International Journal of the Addictions* 16(8):1357–1372.

_____, and M. Lerner. 1974. "Occupational Skills and Life-Styles of Narcotic Addicts." *Sociological Aspects of Drug Dependence*. Cleveland, Oh.: CRC Press.

O'Donnell, John A. 1968. "Diffusion of the Intravenous Technique Among Narcotic Addicts in the U.S." *Journal of Health and Social Behavior* 9:120–130.

_____. 1969. *Narcotic Addicts in Kentucky*. Washington, D.C.: U.S. Government Printing Office.

Oetting, E. R. and Fred Beauvais. 1988. "Common Elements in Youth Drug Abuse: Peer Clusters and Other Psychosocial Factors," in Stanton Peele (ed.) *Visions of Addiction*. Lexington, Mass.: Lexington Books.

Parsons, Talcott. 1951. *The Social System*. New York: Free Press.

Pascarelli, Emil F. and William Fisher. 1974. "Drug Dependence in the Elderly". *International Journal of Aging and Human Development*. 5(4) 347–356.

Peele, Stanton. 1985. *The Meaning of Addiction*. Lexington, Mass.: Lexington Books.

_____. 1988. *Visions of Addiction*. Lexington, Mass.: Lexington Books.

Platt, Jerome J. 1986. *Heroin Addiction: Theory, Research, and Treatment*. 2nd ed. Malabar, Fla.: Krieger.

Pottieger, Anne E. 1981. "Sample Bias in Drugs/Crime Research: an Empirical Study" in James Inciardi (ed.) *The Drugs and Crime Connection*. Beverly Hills: Sage.

Preble, Edward and J. J. Casey. 1969. "Taking Care of Business—The Heroin Users Life on the Street." *International Journal of the Addictions* 4:1–24.

_____ and T. Miller. 1977. "Methadone, Wine and Welfare," in R. S. Weppner (ed.) *Street Ethnography*. Beverly Hills, Calif.: Sage.

Rado, S. 1933. "The Psychoanalysis of Pharmacothymia (Drug Addiction)." *Psychoanalytic Quarterly* 2:1–23.

Rainwater, Lee. 1970. *Behind Ghetto Walls*. Chicago, Ill.: Aldine.

Ray, Marsh. 1964. "The Cycle of Abstinence and Relapse Among Heroin Addicts," in Howard S. Becker (ed.) *The Other Side*. New York: Free Press.

Robins, Lee N. 1973. *The Vietnam Drug User Returns*. Washington, D.C.: U.S. Government Printing Office.

_____. 1979. "Addict Careers," in R. Dupont, A. Goldstein, J. O'Donnell, and B. Brown (eds.) *Handbook on Drug Abuse*. Washington, D.C.: National Institute on Drug Abuse.

_____ and G. E. Murphy. 1967. "Drug Use in a Normal Population of Young Negro Men." *American Journal of Public Health*. 57: 1580–1596.

Rodman, Hyman. 1963. "The Lower Class Valve Stretch", *Social Forces*. XLII(2)CDEC: 205–215.

Rosenbaum, Marsha. 1981. *Women on Heroin*. New Brunswick, N.J.: Rutgers University Press.

Schasre, E. 1966. "Cessation Patterns Among Neophyte Heroin Users." *International Journal of the Addictions* 1:23–32.

Schur, Edwin C. 1971. *Labeling Deviant Behavior*. New York: Harper and Row.

Shaffer, J. W., D. N. Nurco, and T. W. Kinlock. 1984. "A New Classification of Narcotic Addicts Based on Type and Extent of Criminal Activity." *Comp. Psychiatry* 25:315–328.

Silbert, Mimi H., Ayala M. Pines and Teri Lynch. 1982. "Substance Abuse and Prostitution." *Journal of Psychoactive Drugs*. 14(3), July-Sept, 193–197.

Simpson, Dwayne and S. B. Sells. 1981. Highlights of the DARP Follow-Up: Research on the Evaluation of Drug Abuse Treatment Effectiveness. Washington, DC: National Institute on Drug Abuse.

Slim, Iceburg. 1969. *Pimp: The Story of My Life*. Los Angeles, Calif.: Holloway.

Smith, R. B. and Richard C. Stephens. 1976. "Drug Use and 'Hustling': A Study of Their Interrelationships," in *Criminology* 14(2). Beverly Hills, Calif.: Sage.

204   THE STREET ADDICT ROLE

Snow, Mary. 1973. "Maturing out of Narcotic Addiction in New York City." *International Journal of Addictions*. 8(6):921–938.

Stack, Carol B. 1974. *All Our Kin: Strategies for Survival in a Black Community*. New York: Harper and Row.

Stephens, Richard C. 1971. "Relapse Among Narcotic Addicts: An Empirical Test of Labelling Theory." Ph.D. dissertation, University of Wisconsin.

———. 1982. "The Concept of 'Self' in Adolescent Drug Abuse Theories." *Youth and Society* 14(2):213–234.

———. 1985. "The Sociocultural View of Heroin Use: Toward a Role Theoretic Model." *Journal of Drug Issues* (Fall) 433–446.

———. 1986. "A Review of Life With Heroin," by Bill Hanson, J. M. Walters, and E. Bovelle. *Journal of Psychoactive Drugs* 18(2):169–170.

———. 1987. *Mind-Altering Drugs: Use, Abuse, and Treatment*. Vol. 9. Beverly Hills, Calif.: Sage.

———. 1990. "Psychoactive Drug Use in the United States Today." *Drugs and Crime Reader* ed. Thomas Mieczkowski. New York: Allyn and Bacon.

——— and E. Cottrell. 1972. "A Follow-Up Study of 200 Narcotic Addicts Committed for Treatment Under the Narcotic Addict Rehabilitation Act (NARA)." *British Journal of Addictions* 67:445–453.

——— and Rosalind D. Ellis. 1975. "Narcotic Addicts and Crime: Analysis of Recent Trends." *Criminology*. Beverly Hills, Calif.: Sage.

——— and Stephen Levine. 1971. "The Street Addict Role." *Psychiatry* 34:351–357.

——— and Stephen Levine. 1973. "Crime and Narcotic Addiction," in Richard E. Hardy and John G. Cull (eds.) *Applied Psychology in Law Enforcement and Correction*. Springfield, Ill.: Charles C. Thomas.

———, Stephen Levine and Wesley Ross. 1976. "Street Addict Values: A Factor Analytic Study." *Journal of Social Psychology* 99:273–281.

——— and Duane McBride. 1976. "Becoming a Street Addict." *Human Organization* 35(1):78–94.

——— and Gerald T. Slatin. 1974. "The Street Addict Role: Toward the Definition of a Type." *Drug Forum* 3(4):375–389.

——— and R. B. Smith. 1976. "Copping and Caveat Emptor: The Street Addict as a Consumer." *Addictive Diseases: An International Journal* 2(4):285–600.

——— and Robert S. Weppner. 1973a. "Legal and Illegal Use of Methadone: One Year Later." *American Journal of Psychiatry* 130:1391–1394.

——— and Robert S. Weppner. 1973b. "Patterns of 'Cheating' Among Methadone Maintenance Patients." *Drug Forum* 2(4):357–366.

Strauss, Anselm. 1959. *Mirrors and Masks*. New York: Free Press.

Stryker, Sheldon. 1980. *Symbolic Interactionism*. Menlo Park, Calif.: Benjamin/Cummings.

——— and E. A. Craft. 1982. "Deviance, Selves and Others, Revisited." *Youth and Society* 14:159–183.

——— and A. S. Macke. 1978. "Status Inconsistency and Role Conflict." *Annual Review of Sociology* 4:57–90.

——— and Richard T. Serpe. 1982. "Committment, Identity Salience, and Role Behavior: Theory and Research Example" in W. C. Ickes and E. Knowles (eds). *Personality, Roles, and Social Behavior*. New York: Springer-Verlag.

Sutter, Alan. 1966. "The World of the Righteous Dope Fiend." *Issues in Criminology* 2(2):177–222.

Thomas, Piri. 1967. *Down These Mean Streets*. New York: Alfred A. Knopf, Inc.

Trebach, Arnold. 1987. *The Great Drug War*. New York: MacMillan.

Turner, Jonathon. *The Structure of Sociological Theory*. Homewood, Ill.: Dorsey Press, 1974.

Turner, Ralph. 1962. "Role Taking: Process vs. Conformity." *Human Behavior*. ed. Arnold M. Rose. Boston: Houghton Mifflin.

_____. 1978. "The Role and the Person." *American Journal of Sociology* 84(1):1–21.

Valentine, Charles A. 1968. *Culture and Poverty.* Chicago, Ill.: University of Chicago Press.

VanSell, Mary, Arthur P. Brief, and Randall S. Schuler. 1981. "Role Conflict and Role Ambiguity: Integration of the Literature and Direction for Future Research." *Human Relation* 34(1):43–71.

Voss, H. L. and Richard C. Stephens. 1973. "Criminal History of Narcotic Addicts." *Drug Forum* 2:191–202.

Waldorf, Dan. 1973. *Careers in Dope.* Englewood Cliffs: Prentice-Hall.

_____. 1976. "Life Without Heroin: Some Social Adjustments During Long-Term Periods of Voluntary Abstention," in Robert Coombs, Lincoln J. Fry and Patricia Lewis (eds.) *Socialization in Drug Abuse.* Cambridge, Mass.: Schenkman.

Weil, Andrew. 1972. *The Natural Mind: A New Way of Looking at Drugs and the Higher Consciousness.* Boston, Mass.: Houghton Mifflin.

Weppner, Robert. 1977. *Street Ethnography.* Beverly Hills, Calif.: Sage.

_____. 1983. *The Untherapeutic Community: Organizational Behavior in a Failed Addiction Treatment Program.* Lincoln, Nebr.: University of Nebraska Press.

_____ and Michael M. Agar. 1971. "Immediate Precursors to Heroin Addiction." *Journal of Health and Social Behavior* 12:10–18.

_____ and Richard C. Stephens. 1973. "The Illicit and Diversion of Methadone on the Street as Related by Hospitalized Addicts." *Journal of Drug Issues.* 3(1):42–47.

_____, Richard C. Stephens, and Harold T. Conrad. 1972. "Methadone: Some Aspects of Its Legal and Illegal Use." *The Journal of Psychiatry* 129(4):111–115.

Winick, Charles. 1962. "Maturing Out of Narcotic Addiction." *Bulletin on Narcotics* 14(5):1–7.

_____. 1974. "Some Aspects of Careers of Chronic Heroin Users," in Eric Josephson and Eleanor E. Carroll (eds.) *Epidemiological and Sociological Approaches.* New York: Hemisphere.

Wrong, Dennis. "The Over-Socialized Conception of Man in Modern Sociology." *American Sociological Review*. 26:183–193.

Zinberg, Norman. 1979. "Non-Addictive Opiate Use" in *Handbook on Drug Abuse*. Robert Dupont, Avron Goldstein and John O'Donnel (eds). Washington, D.C.: National Institute on Drug Abuse.

————. 1984. *Drug, Set, and Setting*. New Haven, Conn.: Yale University Press.

————, R. C. Jacobson, and W. M. Harding. 1975. "Social Situations and Rituals as a Basis of Drug Abuse Prevention." *American Journal of Drug and Alcohol Abuse* 2:165–182.

————, W. M. Harding, and M. Winkeller. 1977. "A Study of Social Regulatory Mechanism in Controlled Illicit Drug Users." *Journal of Drug Issues* 7:117–133.

Name Index

Agar, Michael
  analysis of street addict toasts, 97
  study of copping, 83
  study of drug use previous to
    heroin use, 74
  study of street addict life, 44
  theory of street addict role, 39
Ageton, S., 116–117
Anderson, Elijah, 132, 138
Ashery, Rebecca, 109

Ball, John C.
  study of narcotics use and crime,
    87, 90
  test of maturation theory, 99
Beauvaise, Fred, 117
Becker, Howard, 32
  role of deviant as master status, 27,
    67
Beschner, George, 62–63
Biernacki, Patrick
  study of addicts who leave the life,
    59, 60, 121
  study of unassisted withdrawal, 107,
    142
  symbolic interaction theory of
    abstinence, 100
  theory of street addict role, 39
Blumer, Herbert, 17, 20
Bovelle, Elliot, 62–63
Brief, Arthur P., 28
Brill, Leon, 166
  push-pull hypothesis of, 100, 101
Brim, Orville G. Jr., 31
Brown, B. S.
  study of cessation of drug use,
    81–82

study of differences between users
    and nonusers, 68
  study of reasons for first use, 71
Brown, C., 39
Brown, Claude, 131
Burroughs, W., 39

Capel, W. C., 101
Caplovitz, David, 93
Casey, J. J., 2
  descriptions of roles in street addict
    life, 49
  theory of street addict role, 39,
    44–45
Chambers, C. D., 162
Cottrell, E., 167
Courtwright, David T., 127
Cox, Terrance, 3
Craft, E. A., 46–47
Craig, S. R., 68
Crawford, Gail
  study of addicts' backgrounds, 71
  study of first heroin use, 73, 74
    nausea and vomiting in, 75
  study of reasons for continued
    heroin use, 77

Delgaty, Robert, 61
Dembo, Richard
  street addict role as deviant career,
    39
  study of adolescent drug users, 46
Desmond, David P.
  study of addict versus nonaddict
    siblings, 70
  study of addicts' employment
    patterns, 94

209

Subject Index

Abstinence, 57–58
  dynamics of, 58–60
  labelling as predictor of relapse,
    57–58
  role conflict as predictor of, 59–60
  role strain as predictor of, 58–59
Addict, street. *See* Street addict
Addiction
  of Civil War veterans, 126
  costs of, as deterrent to drug use,
    162, 163, 180–181
  as deviant lifestyle, 2–3
  as escape, 2
  as extension of normal learning
    processes, 2
  legal risks in, 163
  Lindesmith's theory of, 34–35
    definition of addiction in, 34
    importance of withdrawal in,
      34–35
  as lower class lifestyle
    effect of Harrison Act on,
      139–140
    influence of peer group in, 138
    as one of few options available,
      137
    overlap of, with other roles,
      138–139
    as reaction to sense of failure,
      137–138
  as mental illness, 2
  psychoanalytic approach to,
    109–110
  of well-off white Southern women,
    125–126
  of white criminals, 126–127
Addiction and Opiates (Lindesmith),
  34–35

Addictive personality, 110–111
Addicts
  crimes committed by, 163
  as deviant, 2
  female. *See* Female addicts
  problems with studies of, 113–114
  psychological characterizations of,
    2, 110
  as rational individuals, 120,
    122–123, 180, 181–182
  in leaving the life, 121
  smokers as, 120, 122–123
  in treatment, 155–156
Adult socialization
  for addicts leaving the life, 181–182
  in Narcotics Anonymous, 153
  street addict role as, 53
  in therapeutic community, 150,
    151, 152
AIDS
  contracted by addicts, 8
  as deterrent to drug use, 180–181
  spread of, among addicts, 1
Anslinger, Harry, 129
Anti-societal viewpoint, 50
  definition of, 47
Authority and Addiction (Brill &
  Lieberman), 166

Burn
  avoiding, in copping, 83, 84
  definition of, 83
  recourse, 84

Character and Social Structure (Gerth
  and Mills), 29

215

importance of social circumstances
in, 73–74, 78
influenced by significant others, 71,
73, 75
role of curiosity in, 72, 73
role of older addict in, 71–72,
72–73
role of peer group in, 72, 73
as unplanned event, 73–74
vomiting in, 75, 76–77
Focal concerns
of lower class, 133
of middle and upper classes, 134

Genetic deficiency theory of heroin
use
criticisms of, 107–108
description of, 106–107
Ghetto-specific complex, 136–137
Great Drug War, The (Trebach), 165,
178

Hallucinogens
types of, 4–5
uses of, 4–5
Hardest Drug, The (Kaplan), 166,
167
Harrison Act
criminal addict subculture resulting
from, 130
description of, 129
economic ramifications of, 130
interpretation of, 129–130
street addict subculture resulting
from, 139–140
Heroin
considered dangerous drug, reasons
for, 7–8
first use of
after previous drug use, 74
euphoria in, 75
importance of social
circumstances in, 73–74, 78

influenced by significant others,
71, 73, 75
role of curiosity in, 72, 73
role of older addict in, 71–72,
72–73
role of peer group in, 72, 73
as unplanned event, 73–74
vomiting in, 75, 76–77
high, description of, 8–9
lack of chronic physiological effects
of, 8
second use of, 76
Heroin addiction. *See also* Heroin use
first addiction, 80–83
and first use, 68–78
honeymoon period, 78–80
leaving the life, 97–101
and second use, 76–78
street addict life in, 83–97, 101,
102–103
timetable in, 7
Heroin maintenance
advantages of, 171, 172
as alternative to methadone
maintenance, 171
in Britain, 170, 172
criticisms of, 171–172
Trebach's argument for, in the U.S.,
170
Heroin Solution, The (Trebach), 170
Heroin use. *See also* Heroin
addiction, Withdrawal
dependent variable
defined, 41, 184nn4–5
extent of use in, 41
economic and social impact of, 89
extent of, and degree of
commitment to street addict
role, 42–43, 51–52
motivation for
avoiding withdrawal, 7
getting high, 7
movement of, into lower-class areas
of cities, 131–132